Y0-GEJ-766

Democratization and the Islamist Challenge in the Arab World

STATE, CULTURE, AND SOCIETY IN ARAB NORTH AFRICA

Series Editors

John P. Entelis, Fordham University

Michael Suleiman, Kansas State University

The states and societies of Arab North Africa have long been neglected in the scholarly literature dealing with the Arab world, the Middle East, and Islam, except in the context of dramatic international events. Yet this region has a rich historical and cultural tradition that offers important insights into the evolution of society, the complexity of cultural life, forms of social interaction, strategies of economic development, and patterns of state formation throughout the developing world. In addition, as the region has assumed more importance in geopolitical terms, both the United States and Europe have become more directly involved in its economics and politics. Few books of a scholarly or policy nature, how-ever, analyze and interpret recent trends and changes in the constellation of relations between regional and global powers. This new series—the first in English to focus exclusively on North Africa—will address important conceptual and policy issues from an interdisciplinary perspective, giving special emphasis to questions of political culture and political economy.

Books in This Series

Democratization and the Islamist Challenge in the Arab World, Najib Ghadbian

Political Ascent: Contemporary Islamic Movements in North Africa, Emad Eldin Shahin

The North African Environment at Risk, edited by Will D. Swearingen and Abdellatif Bencherifa

Polity and Society in Contemporary North Africa, edited by I. William Zartman and William Mark Habeeb

36201396

Democratization and the Islamist Challenge in the Arab World

Najib Ghadbian

WITHDRAWN

BP
63
A4
A7241
1997

SLC 6/16/97

WestviewPress
A Division of HarperCollins*Publishers*

OHIO UNIVERSITY
LIBRARY

State, Culture, and Society in Arab North Africa

All rights reserved. Printed in the United States of America. No part of this publication may be reproduced or transmitted in any form or by any means, electronic or mechanical, including photocopy, recording, or any information storage and retrieval system, without permission in writing from the publisher.

Copyright © 1997 by Westview Press, A Division of HarperCollins Publishers, Inc.

Published in 1997 in the United States of America by Westview Press, 5500 Central Avenue, Boulder, Colorado 80301-2877, and in the United Kingdom by Westview Press, 12 Hid's Copse Road, Cumnor Hill, Oxford OX2 9JJ

Typeset by Letra Libre

Library of Congress Cataloging-in-Publication Data
Ghadbian, Najib
Democratization and the Islamist challenge in the Arab world / Najib Ghadbian.
p. cm.— (State, culture, and society in Arab North Africa)
Includes bibliographical references and index.
ISBN 0-8133-2784-9
1. Islam and politics—Arab countries. 2. Islam and state—Arab countries. 3. Arab countries—politics and government—1945– 4. Islam—20th century. I. Title. II. Series.
BP63.A4A7247 1997
320.917'4927'948—dc21 97-411
CIP

The paper used in this publication meets the requirements of the American National Standard for Permanence of Paper for Printed Library Materials Z39.48-1984.

10 9 8 7 6 5 4 3 2 1

For my intellectual companion, Mohja

Contents

Tables and Illustrations

Preface

Serious democratization measures have occurred in the Arab world since the mid-1980s, particularly in Egypt, Jordan, Algeria, and Yemen. The rise of Islamic movements ("fundamentalism" or "political Islam") has coincided with this push toward democracy. Islamists have participated in and benefitted from the democratization process, especially in countries that allowed free elections (e.g., Jordan and Algeria). Why has democratization reached an impasse in the Arab world? What is the intersection of democratization with the rise of the Islamists? What are the prospects for democracy in the current contexts of the Arab world?

This work explores these questions in terms of identity struggle as manifested in the conflict between ruling elites, secularists, and their Islamist challengers. In contexts where the conflict over collective identity has subsided and some sort of tentative compromise, if not total agreement, about the role of Islam in the public domain has been achieved, the process of democratization has advanced. Countries whose governments have allowed Islamists limited participation, and in which Islamists have agreed to work within the system, are closer to democratization than countries whose governments have refused to recognize them at all and in which Islamists are correspondingly more radical. The decision to accommodate diversity procedurally is achieved best if it comes first from political leaders and proceeds gradually. Second, where the sides are sharply polarized over collective identity to the point of attempting change by violent means, the outcome is generally not democratic rule but another form of authoritarianism, whether in Islamist or secularist form. Third, democratization has not advanced in places where major local or international interests are most threatened by the rise of new forces, namely Islamists.

Part One lays out the methodology and provides historical background, tracing the Arab world's struggle with collective identity and how it has influenced democratization. Part Two begins by surveying the democratization measures that have taken place since 1980 and charting the rise of the Islamist challenge. Here I describe the nature of the Islamist challenge, analyze the factors behind its rise, discuss the Islamists' agendas, and examine Islamist concepts of and actual experiences with democracy. Part Three consists of two case studies, one of Egypt's coercion and containment of Islamists and the other of Jordan's milder experience with Islamists. I conclude by discussing the prospects for democracy in the Arab world.

For translation of Arabic words, I have used the simple system of the *International Journal of Middle East Studies*, with some modifications following those of Albert Hourani in *A History of the Arab Peoples*. Thus, the `*ayn* is indicated by an inverted apostrophe (`) and the *hamzah* is indicated by an apostrophe (') only if they come in the middle of a word. Second, the definite article *al-* is prefixed to an Arabic name only the first time the name is used. Third, doubled vowels in the middle of a word are indicated by *iyya* or *uwwa*. Finally, words or names which have a familiar English transliteration are used in the familiar form, such as "Nasser" of Egypt rather than "Nasir," except that official spellings are used for "Makkah" and "Madinah."

Najib Ghadbian
New Brunswick, New Jersey

Acknowledgments

The writing of a book is never an individual work. So many people, including those listed here, have helped and have my earnest gratitude.

I would like to thank my professors at The Graduate School, CUNY: Dankwart Rustow, Ervand Abrahamian, Jacquiline Braveboy-Wagner, Kenneth P. Erickson, Howard Lentner, and W. Ofuatey-Kodjoe. I am grateful to my colleagues at The Graduate School who discussed these ideas with me. Professor John Entelis generously read the manuscript and urged me to seek publication. Laura Parsons, Barbara Ellington, and Patricia Heinicke at Westview have provided patient professional attention to the manuscript. Thanks to Jon Brooks and Andrew Davis at Letra Libre for typesetting.

I wish also to thank all those who granted me interviews in Jordan, Egypt, Sudan, Saudi Arabia, and the United States, and those who kindly helped me arrange the interviews.

I thank my friends who provided good-humor and computer-literate advice at key points.

My family has supported me in many ways throughout the writing. My parents, sisters, brothers, and in-laws encouraged and implored me to finish.

Most of all, I want to thank my wife, Mohja Kahf, for reading, responding, disagreeing, editing, reading again, and otherwise contributing lovingly to this work.

N. G.

PART ONE

Charting Democracy in the Arab World

1

Studying Democratization in the Arab World

After making headway in many countries, efforts to democratize have reached something of an impasse in the Arab world. Discussions about the extent to which this can be attributed to cultural, religious, political, or socioeconomic factors have been inconclusive; some have revived the old imperialist arguments about the inherent unreadiness of certain peoples for self-representation; some border on the blatantly racist.[1]

Egypt, Syria, Iraq, Lebanon, Sudan, and other Arab states made attempts at liberal democracy in the postindependence years. Most of those early experiments soon failed. In Lebanon, however, democracy lasted until the eruption of civil war in 1975, and in Sudan, three intervals of democratic government alternated with military rule. Despite these mixed results, many democratic values—such as the belief in the accountability of leaders and in a more inclusive process of decision-making—retained their status as ideals. These values have deep cultural roots in the Arab world as well as powerful contemporary resonance. Regimes of varied ideological colorings have felt obliged to use democratic vocabulary. One of Gamal Abdul Nasser's six-point programs advocated the establishment of "healthy" democratic life. Ba`thist ideology claimed democracy as a goal. The official name of South Yemen, an authoritarian Marxist-Leninist state, contained a double emphasis on democracy for good measure: the People's Democratic Republic of Yemen.

It was not until the early 1980s, however, that serious steps toward democracy occurred in a notable number of Arab countries: Egypt, Tunisia, Algeria, Jordan, Kuwait, and Yemen. These steps reached their summit after the collapse of the Communist Bloc, perhaps best symbolized by the destruction of the Berlin wall. In the face of such a powerful blow to authoritarianism and the waning of Soviet military support, even the most despotic regimes in the Arab world—Syria and Iraq—were forced to adopt some measures, however cosmetic, to camouflage their rule with democratic trappings.

A few years after this latest wave of democratization began, only Jordan and Yemen have proceeded with democratization, while Egypt and Tunisia have reversed course. In Algeria, the military abruptly ended the democratic experiment in early 1992.

Recent studies have been skeptical about the prospects for democracy in the region in light of another trend, the rise of Islamic movements (sometimes called "Islamic fundamentalism"). Islamist groups seemed to ride the crest of every democratization wave and to gain strength with every opening for change. It is this development which has prompted intellectuals and policy-makers to question whether Arab peoples are "ready" for democracy or whether democracy is even desirable in this area. To many of these political analysts, the involvement in politics of religion in general and Islam in particular is antithetical to democracy. Can democracy develop in an Islamic cultural-political context?

Islamic resurgence, reflected in the rise of Islamist groups in the political arena, poses a serious challenge to the ruling elites in most Arab states. Islamist groups have won ground in each of those Arab countries that allowed free elections, especially in Jordan and Algeria, and Islamist groups have produced an opposition movement in those states that refused to open up their popular bases, such as Syria. It was the rise of Islamists that jolted ruling elites to reconsider whether they should continue down the democratic road when that course seemed to put their own survival at risk.

Why has democratization reached an impasse in the Arab world? What are the positions of Islamist movements toward democracy? What are the prospects for continued transition toward democracy, in light of the Islamist challenge?

Defining Democracy, Arab, and Islamist

In this study, the institutional or procedural aspect of democracy is the defining factor, following Joseph Schumpeter, who defines democracy as "the institutional arrangement for arriving at political decisions in which individuals acquire the power to decide by means of a competitive struggle for the people's vote."[2] Procedural elements being foremost, democracy is the form of government that meets the following criteria:[3]

1. Free and periodic competition between at least two candidates occurs for all effective decision-making positions. The end result is a peaceful transition of government.
2. A high degree of political participation in the election of leaders exists. The entire adult population is allowed to participate in elections; suffrage is universal.

3. There are guarantees of human and civil rights and liberties, such as freedom of expression, freedom of the press, freedom to join and form political parties, etc.
4. The leaders are held accountable to the public as long as they hold office. This requires the existence of a means of removing leaders from office if they violate the law.

Democracy, as defined above, is an ideal form of government. Thus a perfect implementation of democracy is rare, even among democratic countries. For instance, the United States suffers from a strikingly low level of participation in national elections[4] and the disproportionate influence of interest groups in the making of decisions. In addition, this definition covers only "political" or "liberal" democracy and omits the view that sees democracy as a social and economic as well as political system. In the view of social democrats, free elections and political pluralism are not enough to make democracy; economic equality must be accessible, or the state must at least be committed to moving the country toward equal economic opportunity for all. Such a view envisions a wider role for the state than that advocated by liberal democrats. The narrow political definition is most relevant in this work. However, the case studies of Egypt and Jordan address the role of economic contexts in the conflict over political participation in the Arab world and acknowledge the potential for further research in that direction.

Although no Arab country has become a full-fledged democracy, some countries have moved closer to democracy than others. This is why we speak of democratization as a transitional process toward fulfillment of some criteria for democracy. Democratization, according to Hudson, "is the process through which the exercise of political power by the state becomes less arbitrary and exclusive."[5] Some scholars distinguish between liberalization and democratization. Liberalization refers to a change which limits the power of the state to intervene in the life of people and allows some freer expression and oppositional activities. Democratization refers more specifically to the process of change toward free elections, popular participation, and freedom of the masses; it is a change toward democratic rule.[6] Huntington, among others,[7] depicts democratization as a prolonged and complex process bringing an end to the nondemocratic regime, establishing the democratic regime, and finally, consolidating the democratic system.[8] While democratization is more far-reaching than liberalization, the transition toward democracy could begin and usually begins when nondemocratic regimes loosen—liberalize—their tight control over the populace, which may or may not lead to democratization. In this book the process of democratization, rather than the ideal of democracy, is the focus.

Although the modest steps taken by Arab regimes might qualify only as liberalizing measures, some of these measures have been serious enough to induce a broad process of change. Algeria, for example, moved from a one-party to a multiparty system—although the process was then halted by military force. Even if some of the modest changes in Arab states—such as restoring parliament or lifting martial law—only qualify as liberalizing measures, the fact that most Arab regimes are under pressure to make more such changes or face deepening legitimacy crises indicates that liberalization is pushing steadily in the direction of democratization.

"The Arab world" refers to those countries which are members in the Arab League.[9] Using the Arab world as a single unit of analysis is significant. Much of the scholarship emerging from the academic and policy-research institutions of the United States and Europe assumes that the divided status of the region precludes speaking of an "Arab world," while most Arab scholars do not hesitate to use this term despite the divisions within the region. This is a reflection of ideological bias on both sides.

One may refer to "the Arab world" without losing sight of the fact that the Arab world is a dynamic entity rather than a static one. As Arab sociologist Halim Barakat points out, "Arab society is not a mere mosaic of sects, ethnic groups, tribes, local communities and regional entities. Rather, it carries within it the potential for both unity and divisiveness." He emphasizes the need to recognize "conditions that constantly pull contemporary Arab society between all sorts of polarities and conflicting orientations: unity versus fragmentation, tradition versus modernity, sacred versus secular, East versus West, local versus national . . . "[10] Still, Barakat entitles the book in which he recognizes all these polarities *The Arab World*.

Taking the Arab world as the broad unit of analysis is justified by empirical and not just ideological reasons. Despite differences among Arab countries, all are governed by authoritarian regimes that are under pressure to democratize, and all have witnessed a rise of Islamic consciousness; these are the two trends examined in this project. The emphasis of this book is on those states that have initiated a democratic opening and later witnessed a deadlock. Two countries will be examined closely: Jordan and Egypt. This approach balances the advantages of breadth of vision, in taking the entire Arab world into account, and specificity, in examining certain states in detail.

The term "Islamist challenge" refers to the pressure generated by movements of Islamic resurgence in the Arab world. These are movements that seek to change their societies by deriving their programs and ideologies from the basic texts of Islam. The term "Islamic fundamentalism" carries connotations from American Protestantism and reduces a wide and complex range of groups and individuals to stereotypes (e.g.

extremists, militants, terrorists) sharpened in past decades in the Western and Arab news media. "Islamist" ("*Islamiyyun*") is what people belonging to Islamic movements call themselves, while "fundamentalist" is what their opponents derisively call them in a foreign tongue. "Fundamentalist," with its judgmental tone and its implications of literalism, antimodernism, and fanaticism, is a term for those who have already made up their minds about all Islamists and is therefore inappropriate for scholarly research.[11] "Islamist" is distinct from "Muslim" in that the former refers to people with a conscious activist agenda while the latter is a nominal identity for people of a gamut of ideological views. The majority of the Arab world is Muslim, while only those with ideologies that call for the implementation of Islam in the public as well as private realms are Islamists.

Beyond Cultural and Economic Explanations

Early theorizing about transition to democracy concentrated on discovering preconditions that supposedly correlate with democracy, such as socioeconomic factors, political culture, regime legitimacy, and external influences.[12] Huntington has compiled a list of twenty-seven propositions or variables that are conducive to democracy, including:

- a market economy
- a strong middle class
- high levels of literacy and education
- Protestantism
- democratic authority structures within social groups, particularly those closely connected to politics
- low levels of political polarization and extremism
- political leaders committed to democracy
- experience as a British colony.[13]

The fact that such factors correlate with democracy does not necessarily mean that they cause it.[14] We need to know how they interact in a specific context in order to explain anything. If we take economic development and civic political culture as two factors which correlate to democracy, and measure them against evidence from the Arab world, the shortcomings of this approach will be apparent.

Economic Development

A classic example of the argument that high per capita income and high literacy levels, as indications of economic development, are strongly correlated to democracy, is Lipset's work.[15] This was part of a body of theorizing which posited that liberal democracy would occur as a result of modernization. Political realities in developing countries refuted this assertion, since modernization, particularly during the 1950s and 1960s, did not necessarily seem to result in increased democratization. The political reality of the Arab world as it modernized not only failed to correspond to this theory, but witnessed the rise of authoritarianism in both its populist and patrimonial forms. Some Arab regimes even fit Hudson's description of "the *Mukhabarat* state," a state based on an extensive secret police apparatus and operating on fear rather than consent.[16]

In contrast, O'Donnell argues that bureaucratic authoritarianism can be expected in the early stages of economic development as an efficient way of dealing with the difficulties of modernization.[17] O'Donnell's argument better explains the existence of such regimes as postindependence Algeria. However, the process of economic development that produced bureaucratic-authoritarianism in the 1960s has also been crucial in the initiation of the democratic movement in the 1980s.

It is plausible that in early stages of economic development authoritarianism is more likely to prevail. As economies become wealthy and complex, it becomes more difficult for authoritarian regimes to maintain tight control; therefore, economic development leads to political openness.[18] Huntington says that economic development leads to the enlargement of middle class and increase of education; these two factors, in turn, create attitudes that are supportive of democracy. Ultimately, however, economic development alone cannot explain the transition toward democracy. Other factors—such as amenable political leadership—must follow for democracy to come about.[19]

Political Culture

Another factor widely used to explain the existence of democracy is political culture—the values, beliefs, and attitudes that support or resist a certain political order. Numerous Western scholars have used this approach to explain the absence of liberalism and democracy in the Arab world. According to one segment of this argument, certain unchanging attributes which supposedly characterize the Arab people, such as duplicity, irrationality, codes of shame and honor, and so forth, are not compatible with democracy.[20] In a survey of literature on Arab political culture and democracy, Lisa Anderson observed "Probably the characteristic of this literature most likely to strike an uninitiated observer is the negative tone of most of the assessments. Not only are Arabs thought to be dismal prospects for democratic politics, but they appear to be fairly dismal people all around: illogical, untrustworthy, passive before domineering rulers, while given to intrigue and violence—all in all, an unsavory lot."[21] Aside from their racist undertones, such approaches are riddled with logical flaws and methodological obscurantism. For example, many of these arguments simultaneously insist that Arab society is hopelessly divided and that one uniform Arab mentality exists.[22]

The second segment of the argument that Arab political culture cannot produce democracy blames the absence of democracy on "Islam" in general. Several writers contrast Protestantism, as the religion favorable to democracy, with others, including Islam, which are supposedly not conducive to democracy. In a widely publicized article, Huntington writes "Islam has not been hospitable to democracy . . . in Islam, for instance, no distinction exists between religion and politics or between the spiritual and the secular." He goes on to say that "political participation was historically an alien concept."[23] Huntington derives this sweeping categorization by simple correlation between Muslim countries and the lack of democracy, rather than by a study of Islamic culture and its relationship to politics in the Middle East.[24]

Despite their shortcomings, works on Arab political culture as an impediment to democracy continue to find publishers and advocates. One prominent scholar on the Middle East claims that democracy has failed in the Arab world because "the idea of democracy is quite alien to the mind-set of Islam."[25] Not only have Arabs been long accustomed to the traditions of autocracy and passive obedience, apparently, but they have only adopted the worst of Western political tradition, that of enlightened absolutism, which makes it questionable if the Arab peoples will ever be able to rid themselves of these evils.

Essentialism and overgeneralization are the obvious pitfalls of this approach. Another problem with the cultural explanation of democracy or its absence is the assumption that beliefs unilaterally influence actions. It is quite possible that the relationship between beliefs and actions is reciprocal. Rustow at least agrees to "allow for the possibility that circumstances may force, trick, lure, or cajole nondemocrats into democratic behavior and that their beliefs may adjust in due course by some process of rationalization and adaptation."[26] Huntington acknowledges in his later work the limits of his earlier cultural explanation, because similar arguments about other cultures have not held up, because a "culture" such as Islam is complex and may contain democratic as well as undemocratic elements, and most of all, because cultures change. A more fruitful way to examine the question of culture is to ask, "What forms of politics might emerge in these countries when economic prosperity begins to interact with Islamic values and traditions?"[27]

Deciding Who the People Are

No single factor is sufficient to explain either the development or the frustration of democracy. Rather, democratization is the result of a combination of causes, a combination which varies from country to country and is likely to vary over time. While certain factors are favorable to democracy, such as high literacy rates and advanced economic development, these factors might be necessary but are not sufficient for the establishment of democracy. It is crucial to maintain a clear distinction between functional and genetic explanations; correlation is not causation.[28]

People or political actors, from among both the leadership and the public, must act to establish or overthrow democratic systems: "Democracies are created not by causes but by causers."[29] Nevertheless, political leaders cannot create democracy if favorable conditions are absent. It is the interaction between favorable socioeconomic, international, and cultural conditions on one hand, and the conscious acts of political leaders and activists on the other, that brings about democratization.

Based on these guidelines, Rustow's model for transition to democracy can be adapted for relevance to the Arab world. The model identifies a background condition and three phases of democratic transition. The background condition is a sense of national unity. In the first phase, there is a persistent and serious conflict leading to the breakdown of the non-democratic regime; a conscious decision to adopt democratic rule occurs in the second phase; finally, there is a consolidation phase in which politicians and the electorate becomes habituated to this type of system (see Figure 1.1).

The one background condition of national unity means simply that most people "have no doubt or mental reservations as to which political community they belong to." As Ivor Jennings puts it, "The people cannot decide until somebody decides who are the people."[30] Countries have had different ways of achieving national unity. Britain and France, for example, achieved national unity before they moved toward democracy. Other nations, such as Germany and Italy, did not resolve the issue of national unity until their violent unification in the late nineteenth century. Two conditions threaten national unity. One is when ethnic or linguistic cleavages among groups within a country lead them to question their national identity, as in the former Yugoslavia. The other case is when a divided nation seeks unification, such as Germany in the mid-nineteenth century. In these two cases, the national question must be settled before moving toward democracy.

As the issue of national unity is resolved, the first phase of transition toward democracy is triggered by a long, indecisive political struggle;

FIGURE 1.1. Rustow's Model for the Transition Toward Democracy

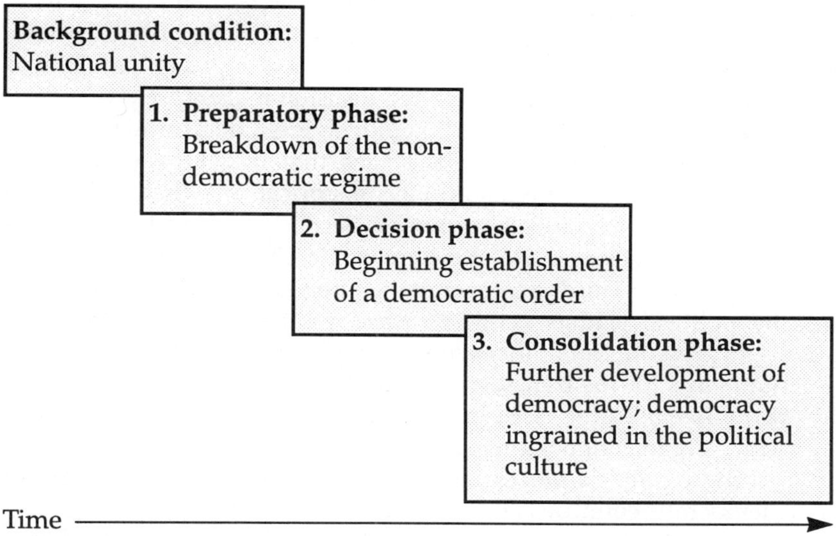

Source: George Sorensen, *Democracy and Democratization* (Boulder, Colo.: Westview, 1993), p. 42. Reprinted by permission.

this is the preparatory phase. The issues of this conflict could be economic or social equity, political rights, or any number of issues worth fighting for. The conflict in this phase is likely to erupt as a result of the rise of a new social group which challenges the dominant class. Although "polarization" is the characteristic of the struggle phase, such polarization must not threaten national unity; otherwise, further national fragmentation is the outcome rather than democracy.

The second phase of the transition is the moment of decision which concludes the preparatory phase, when "deliberate decision on the part of political leaders to accept the existence of diversity in unity and, to that end, to institutionalize some crucial aspect of democratic procedure."[31] This part of the transition process indicates the vital role political leaders play. It is understandable for rising groups to advocate democracy as a means of access to power. It is also reasonable to assume that for members of the ruling elite to open up the system, they must perceive this step as serving their interests. The decision to adopt some democratic procedures, to widen suffrage for example, can lead to consequences unintended by the makers of this decision.

The final phase in the transition toward democracy is that of habituation, in which both politicians and constituents accept and become familiar with the democratic rule. This is also the consolidation phase, which, according to Juan Linz "is one in which none of the major political actors, parties, or organized interests, forces or institution or group has claim to veto the action of democratically elected decision makers."[32]

Three points are in order about this model. First, democratization is a complex process involving various stages that might overlap. These phases do not follow a predetermined historical law that unfolds in exactly the same way in all countries. Second, the model identifies national unity or a clear sense of collective identity as the sole prerequisite for democracy. Third, democratization begins as a result of a choice made by political leaders acting to preserve their own interests as a response to pressure from other groups. Conflict rather than consensus is the central basis for the transition to democracy. In a later work, Rustow adds two other political essentials of democracy, asserting that democracy's multi-organizational imperative is a politically neutral state as well as two or more political parties, and that international efforts to support newly democratic countries are also a factor.[33]

Democratization is held back in the Arab world by the unresolved conflict over collective identity, and complicated by the interference of powerful local and international forces committed to preserving the status quo. Collective identity, "the sharing of essential elements that define the character and orientation of people and affirm their common needs, interests, and goals with reference to joint action" is never a frozen, determined quality; there is always an element of flux about it. Neither is it a unitary, homogenous quality; there is always multiplicity and hybridity in it.[34] Nevertheless, some minimum level of consensus about collective identity must coalesce before a people can come together as a democratic nation. The development of national identity in the Arab world was delayed first by the Ottoman Empire until early this century, and after that by Western domination.[35]

The conflict over collective identity is connected to the major questions that the Arab peoples have faced since independence, such as: How should current national borders dividing the Arab world into over twenty countries be addressed? How should the Arab-Israeli conflict be resolved? What is the role of religion (particularly Islam) in the structuring of society and polity? How should economic wealth, especially oil, be divided? The collective identity crisis has not happened and is not happening in a vacuum, but within the framework of these specific issues.

Three responses to the issue of political fragmentation have emerged. *Qutriyya*, or loyalty to the existing states, solidified over the decades as the postcolonial borders between Arab states proved durable. *Qutriyya* is particularly manifest during Arab-Arab disputes, such as the second Gulf war. *Qawmiyya*, or pan-Arabism, dismisses existing states as artificial and seeks Arab unity. This trend was strongest from the 1950s to the 1970s. Finally, there is regionalism, an emphasis on regional unity, such as "greater Syria," "greater Maghreb" (Morocco, Mauritania, Tunisia, Libya, and Algeria), or the Gulf (al- Khalij) states (those in the Gulf Cooperation Council).

The role of Islam is highly contested. Secularists see Islam as a historical factor but insist that the exclusion of religion from the political realm is a precondition for development and modernization. Islamists see Islam as the frame of reference for organizing political life. However, these seemingly conflicting ideological positions sometimes overlap in practice. This is because secularism is not a substantive political ideology in itself but a component of several differing ideologies, including communism, socialism, and Arab nationalism. Secular shading is gradual and shifting; some Arab nationalists are extremely secular, while others give more weight to Islam in their vision of politics. In the practical terms of political coalitions, therefore, an Arab nationalist may have as much in common with Islamists on one hand as with secular political allies on the other.

The question of plurality versus unity dominated the identity struggle in the Arab world for almost two decades, from the 1950s to the 1970s. The emphasis was on Arab unity as the key to solving the rest of the Arab world's problems. For Arab unity, and for economic development, democracy had to be temporarily sacrificed.[36] Arab leaders and intellectuals used the same arguments on which socialists and communists worldwide relied to legitimize the trade-off of individual freedoms and democratic participation for social equity and economic development. Justice, national integrity, including the restoration of Palestinian rights, and basic physical quality of life for everyone had to come before such luxuries as free expression, the argument went. The (pan-Arab) nation had to come together and defend itself against external dangers before niceties like oppositional parties could be considered.

Today the terms of the argument are reversed, and there is growing agreement that the larger problems of the Arab world cannot be solved unless some level of democratic participation is achieved. At least today Arab intellectuals, the Arab nationalists among them of particular significance, reject the idea that democracy must be traded off for anything, be it Arab unity, economic development, or the restoration of Palestinian rights. Thus, the debate over the legitimacy of the Arab states in their existing borders has subsided. There is general acknowledgement that these divisions are durable for the present and cannot be erased by military force from above.

At the same time, reports of the death of the idea of Arab unity have been greatly exaggerated. It has simply altered its form from a simplistic dream to a pragmatic realization that the present borders of the Arab world will change only gradually, through long-term economic integration (the European Community model is relevant here), through the increased circulation of people, ideas, and goods, and, decidedly, through the participation and consent of the masses. Today, the major political forces, including the Islamists, work within the arena of the existing states, acknowledging the practical primacy of local concerns.

The debate in the 1990s is over the role of Islam in politics. Islam was always a component of Arab nationalism, but a secondary or tertiary one. Islam came to the forefront as a political force after the failure of Arab nationalism to achieve success with its platform. Islamist movements pose a challenge to authoritarian leaders who already suffer from a conspicuous lack of legitimacy. Two elements of power for Islamists are their popularity and the fact that they push for democratic openings in existing systems at a time when people want any change at all from authoritarian rule. Islamist popularity is grounded in an array of social groups with wide bases in Arab societies: students, the young, professionals, the urban poor, etc. Islamists push for change because, in every Arab country except Sudan (and that exception due to relatively recent change), they are in opposition.

There are two camps of opponents to the Islamists: ruling elites and most secularists. As for the ruling elites, despite their defensive need to prove legitimacy by granting some liberalizing measures, they hold the coercive apparatus for repressing Islamist opposition and, in most cases, are not reluctant to use it.

When ruling elites in some Arab countries allowed limited democratic openings, it was Islamist groups which benefitted from these openings. In every election with some degree of freedom and fairness, Islamists gained ground. It is this development which has led ruling elites, secular intellectuals, and others, including many in the West, to reconsider whether democracy is a good thing in the Arab world. As one observer puts it, "Islamic revivalism has often been seen and experienced as a direct threat to the ideas, beliefs, practices, and interests of Muslim secular elites as well as Western governments and multinational corporations."[37] The ruling elites have responded in a variety of ways to Islamist advances, ranging from allowing Islamists to participate in the political process to harsh repression. Almost every Arab government today is entangled in a debate over the role *shari`a* (Islamic law) should play in public life. This new conflict, mainly between secular ruling elites and Islamists, has hampered the democratization process in most Arab countries.

Egypt is a good showcase for this shift in the collective identity and its ramifications for democratization. Loyalty to the idea of Egypt (Egyptian nationalism) was strong before Nasser came to power. Egypt had a parliamentary system with intense friction between the palace and leaders of nationalist parties, and constant manipulation and interference by the British occupiers. The old regime was superficially a democracy, one which, when destroyed by Nasser and his Free Officers, found few mourners. Under Nasser, Arab nationalism or pan-Arabism dominated popular loyalties with total suspension of democracy for the sake of Arab unity, socialism, and the liberation of Palestine. Then Anwar Sadat came with a different mix of ideas and a return to Egyptianism. Sadat, who was always *In Search of Identity*,[38] died at the hands of radical Islamists for isolating Egypt from the rest of the Arab world and signing a separate peace treaty with Israel. Under Husni Mubarak, Islamists have done well in elections despite widespread fraud by the government. Having failed to further democratize and to solve the country's economic problems, Mubarak's government today is under attack from radical Islamists and under pressure from moderate Islamists to adopt an "Islamic solution." The government has found ways to co-opt some Islamists by promoting token "Islamic" policy concessions, suppressing radical elements, and occasionally tolerating moderates, without allowing them to function as a legal party. Egypt has witnessed minor warfare between radical Islamists and the regime throughout the 1990s. The regime is dominated by an elite that feels threatened ideologically by an Islamist rise to power. Democratization, in the meanwhile, is put on hold until this struggle is resolved. All things considered, the regime of Mubarak has not been less authoritarian than those of his predecessors. On the contrary, its record of human rights violations and death penalties against regime opponents has been the worst.

Unlike in Egypt, most political forces in Jordan have reached a working consensus on collective identity. The Jordanian monarchy has succeeded so far in including Islamists in the political process, but within bounds that do not challenge the power of the king. Islamists have shown willingness and skill in working within those procedures of democracy which have been instituted. The question remains, will the monarchy relinquish as much power as the progress of democratization will demand?

The conflict between Islamists and governments has been a shaper of the democratization process in these two countries. How has this process unfolded and what does it mean for democracy in the Arab world?

Notes

1. For example, Raphael Patai, *The Arab Mind* (New York, NY: Charles Scribner's Sons, 1973) and Elie Kedourie, *Democracy and Arab Political Culture* (Washington, DC: The Washington Institute for Near East Policy, 1992).

2. *Capitalism, Socialism, and Democracy*, 2nd ed. (New York, NY: Harper, 1947), p. 269.

3. See Robert Dahl, *Polyarchy* (New Haven, CT: Yale University Press, 1991); Samuel Huntington, "The Modest Meaning of Democracy" in Robert Pastor, ed., *Democracy in America* (New York, NY: Holmes & Meier, 1989).

4. Turn-out in presidential elections is around 50% (55% in 1992) and is even lower in congressional and local elections. See, for example, Milton C. Cummings, Jr. and David Wise, *Democracy Under Pressure: An Introduction to the American Political System*, 7th ed. (Fort Worth, TX: Harcourt Brace Jovanovich College Publishers, 1993), p. 309.

5. Michael Hudson, "Democratization and the Problem of Legitimacy in Middle East Politics," *MESA Bulletin*, Vol. 22, No. 2, 1988, p. 157.

6. See, for example, Augustus Richard Norton, "The Future of Civil Society in the Middle East," *Middle East Journal*, Vol. 47, No. 2, Spring 1993.

7. Dankwart Rustow describes a similar process in "Transition to Democracy," *Comparative Politics*, No. 2, 1970. See also George Sorensen, *Democracy and Democratization* (Boulder, CO: Westview Press, 1993).

8. Samuel Huntington, *The Third Wave* (Norman, OK: University of Oklahoma Press, 1991), p. 9.

9. The twenty-two members of the Arab League are: Algeria, Bahrain, Comoros Islands, Djibouti, Egypt, Iraq, Jordan, Kuwait, Lebanon, Libya, Mauritania, Morocco, Oman, Palestine, Qatar, Saudi Arabia, Somalia, Sudan, Syria, Tunisia, United Arab Emirates, and Yemen.

10. Halim Barakat, *The Arab World* (Berkeley, CA: University of California Press, 1993), p. xii.

11. For further explanation of why "fundamentalism" is not useful, see John Esposito, *The Islamic Threat: Myth or Reality?* (New York, NY: Oxford University Press, 1992), pp. 7–8, and Ervand Abrahamian, *Khomeinism: Essays on the Islamic Republic* (Berkeley, CA: University of California Press, 1993), pp. 13–17.

12. For a review of literature on the pre-conditions for democratic transition, see Dankwart Rustow, "Transition to Democracy," *Comparative Politics*, No. 2, 1970, and Samuel Huntington, "Will More Countries Become Democratic?" *Political Science Quarterly*, Vol. 99, No. 2, 1984.

13. Huntington, *The Third Wave*, p. 37–38.

14. Rustow, "Transition to Democracy," p. 346.

15. Seymour Lipset, "Some Social Requisites of Democracy: Economic Development and Political Legitimacy." *American Political Science Review*, Vol. 53, No. 1, 1959.

16. Hudson, "Democratization . . . ," p. 160.

17. Guillermo O'Donnell, *Modernization and Bureaucratic Authoritarianism* (Berkeley, CA: University of California Press, 1973).

18. David Apter makes this point, cited in D. Rustow and K. Erickson, *Comparative Political Dynamics: Global Research Perspectives* (New York, NY: Harper Collins, 1991), p. 445.

19. Huntington, *The Third Wave*, p. 315.

20. Some of the more notorious examples are Patai's *The Arab Mind* and David Pryce-Jones' *The Closed Circle: An Interpretation of the Arabs* (New York, NY: Harper and Row, 1989).

21. Lisa Anderson, "Democracy in the Arab World: A Critique of the Political Culture Approach," paper presented at the Conference on Political Liberalization and Democratization in the Arab World, McGill University, May 7–8, 1993, p. 20.

22. Barakat, *The Arab World*, p. 15.

23. Huntington, "Will More Countries Become Democratic?" p. 208.

24. Huntington cites only one source as evidence: Daniel Pipes, *In the Path of God: Islam and Political Power* (New York, NY: Basic Books, 1983). The source itself is problematic. Pipes is not a recognized expert on Islam.

25. Kedourie, *Democracy and Arab Political Culture*, p. 1.

26. Rustow, "Transition to Democracy," p. 345.

27. Huntington, *The Third Wave*, p. 315.

28. See Rustow's "Transition to Democracy," Huntington's *The Third Wave*, and Sorensen's *Democracy and Democratization*.

29. Huntington, *The Third Wave*, p. 107

30. Quoted by Rustow, "Transition to Democracy," p. 351.

31. Ibid., p. 355.

32. Quoted in Sorensen, *Democracy and Democratization*, p. 45.

33. Dankwart Rustow, "Dictatorship to Democracy: The Political Transition." Roundtable on Global Change, UNDP, Development Study Programme, Bucharest, Romania, 1992.

34. Barakat, *The Arab World*, p. 32.

35. Rustow, "Arab Perceptions of History and the Question of Identity," in Stanley Renshon, ed., *The Political Psychology of the Gulf War* (Pittsburgh, PA: University of Pittsburgh Press, 1993), p. 24.

36. For a thorough discussion of this trade-off, see a volume of symposium proceedings entitled *al-Dimoqratiyya wa Huquq al-Insan fil Watan al-`Arabi* (Democracy and Human Rights in the Arab World), edited by Research Group Members (Cairo: Dar al-Mustaqbal al-'Arabi, 1993).

37. Esposito, *The Islamic Threat*, p. 10.

38. This is the title of his autobiography.

2

Identity and Democracy: A History

The Rise and Decline of the Arabo-Islamic Nation

In the history of the Arab peoples, the turning point in the nascence of Arab identity was the emergence of Islam. Although the Arabs had political structures before Islam, some of which lasted until the fifth century C.E., the period that preceded Islam was characterized by internecine strife and fragmentation over water and pasturage disputes.[1] In a harsh, hot climate with scarce water, people relied on the tribe, the main social unit, in their struggle for survival. Any sense of belonging or identity was centered on the tribe. In fact, the harshest punishment in pre-Islamic Arab society was to be disowned by one's tribe.

Beginning in 610 C.E., the Prophet Muhammad began to preach a religion called Islam. Islam not only provided the tribes of Arabia with a sense of mission in the world but united them in one political unit. The Prophet and his successors, the caliphs, initiated a process of nation-building—no simple task considering the deep-rooted tribalism it had to overcome. Islam "replaced diversity and fragmentation with unity of religious belief; it rejected the divisive clannishness of the tribes and in its place established the bond of the creed; it cast aside tribal customs and upheld new values and standards, a common goal in life and the fundamental principles of a comprehensive system of religious law."[2]

Islam called its followers an *umma* (community or nation)[3] linked by faith rather than descent or kinship. In order to succeed in the process of building a nation based on new principles, Islam was direct and explicit. The Qur'an refers often to the concept of *umma*, as does the first document drafted after the historic migration of the Prophet to Madinah and the establishment of the Islamic state. In this document, the first item defines the believers: "This is a contract from the Prophet Muhammad, the Messenger of God, between the believers and Muslims of Quraysh [the tribe of the Prophet] and the people of Yathrib with them; verily they are one nation (*umma*) unique beside all the people." This document also distinguishes between the community of believers (the *umma*) and those non-Muslims, especially Christians and Jews, who had a right to live as equals in the Muslim nation. The document refers to the Jews of Madinah as "a nation with (*ma`*) the Muslims," rather than a nation "from" (*min*) the Muslims.[4] The term "with," (*ma`*) denotes alliance between two bodies whereas *min* here would denote simultaneity or overlapping of identity. This points to the religious basis of political identity; the Jews living within the political structure of the Muslim state constituted a community allied with that state.

In the community's effort to build a new nation, the loyalty of the believers was declared to belong to God, to his Prophet, and to the community of believers. However, Islam did not suppress other loyalties, such as tribal loyalty, as long as they did not conflict with or supersede loyalty to the faith. The fact that Arabic was the language of the Qur'an confirmed the status of the language, and Arabization accompanied the spread of Islam. Because Islam required every Muslim to understand the Qur'an (rather than assigning the responsibility for textual knowledge to a priesthood), the Arabic language was given a secure place and a standardized form for the new community. As Islam spread outside the Arabian peninsula, Arabic spread with it and soon became the *lingua franca* of a wide geographic area. The Prophet defined an Arab linguistically rather than racially, thus shifting the weight from ethnicity and race to culture. Arabic became the mother-tongue and "Arab" the primary form of self-identification for a widening circle of peoples, from the Arabian peninsula northward to Bilad al-Sham and Iraq[5] and westward to Egypt and al-Maghreb (the Islamic West). Arabic "became the medium of a culture which incorporated elements from the traditions of peoples absorbed into the Muslim world, and expressed itself in literature and in systems of law, theology, and spirituality."[6] Islam and Islamization spread further than Arabization, to Persia, India, Anatolia, into sub-Saharan Africa, and later, further still. In the core areas where Islamization and Arabization occurred to the same degree, however, a construct of a relatively homogenous collective identity developed over time. There the Arabic language served as a cultural bond between the Muslim majority and the non-Muslim minorities, particularly the Arab Christian communities. At the same time, the common bond of Islamic religion helped create a place for ethnolinguistic minorities who lived within the Arabo-Islamic heartland, such as the Kurds.

The political framework of the *umma* was established during the life of the Prophet. The Qur'an and the *Sunna* (the practice and sayings of the Prophet) together served as the constitution of the Islamic state. The Prophet himself was the head of this state, and, following the Qura'nically mandated principle of *shura* (deliberative consultation), relied on a group of advisors in conducting public affairs. After the death of their Prophet, Muslims founded the caliphate as the main political institution of the *umma*, based on the following principles:[7]

1. The caliph was to be chosen by the *umma*. The manner of choosing was not specified. However, the oath of allegiance was to be a contract between the *umma* and the caliph.
2. Decisions were to be reached by deliberative consultation (*shura*).
3. The ultimate purpose of governance was to establish justice.
4. The *umma* was the source of legislation, but limited by Islamic law (*shari`a*). The caliph was to be obeyed and supported as long as he upheld *shari`a*.

While the first four caliphs (632–661 C.E./11–40 A.H.) were understood by the community as having observed these principles, a gap between principles and reality developed with the coming of the Umayyad dynasty (661–750 C.E./41–132 A.H.). First, the Umayyads violated the principle of election of the caliph by introducing hereditary succession as the means of transfer of power. While Islamic principles such as consultation and justice remained important in theory, Umayyad caliphs were increasingly despotic. Jurists and legal scholars were anxious to save the institution of the caliphate and avoid internecine strife (*fitna*). Their response was to bring theory in line with practice by accepting the principle of hereditary succession and justifying the absolute powers of the caliph.[8]

Power changed from Umayyad to Abbasid hands in 749 C.E. (132 A.H.), and the capital moved from Damascus to Baghdad. Along with the spread of Islam and rapid Arabization, the Abbasid epoch witnessed the increased participation of non-Arabs in both political and military life. However, by the tenth century C.E., the institution of the caliphate was weakening and rival caliphs appeared in Spain and Egypt. Although the Abbasid caliph in Baghdad continued to be the titular head of state until the thirteenth century, there were three de facto political regions: Iraq together with Iran, Egypt and Syria, and the Maghreb. Mongol invasions during the thirteenth and fourteenth centuries accelerated the fragmentation of the eastern Arab world. In spite of this division, the "Arabic-speaking parts of the Muslim world had maintained social and cultural unity and showed similarities from one region to another."[9] Moreover, the community maintained its unity and the authority of the *shari`a*, religious law, remained a fundamental concept. The break-up of the caliphate and the emergence of quasi-independent states and principalities accompanied the end of the political unity of the Arabic-speaking peoples.

During the fifteenth and sixteenth centuries, most Arab lands came under the rule of the Ottomans, a dynasty established by Turks originating from Anatolia. After taking Istanbul as their capital in 1453 C.E., the Ottomans were quickly able to expand their rule all the way from Iraq to Algeria. Thus, the Arabic-speaking world regained its unity, but this time under the banner of the Ottoman Empire, a bureaucratic state holding many regions under one administrative system. The Ottoman Empire, in the first two centuries of its rule over Arab regions, preserved the status of *shari`a* and protected the frontiers of the Arab world. This gave the Ottoman Empire legitimacy in the eyes of its Arab subjects.

The prestige of the Arabic language waned under Ottoman rule. As Ottoman Turkish became the language of administration and of the military, Arabic was used mainly by the religious strata. Arabic *belle lettres* deteriorated and the period is considered one of general stagnation for Arab intellectual life (although a few Arab literary historians have disputed this widely-held view).

By the early eighteenth century, the Ottoman Empire itself entered a period of decline characterized by two simultaneous processes. One is that local ruling families became more powerful and autonomous at the expense of the central empire. The other is that increasingly powerful European nations began pursuing their own interests inside Ottoman lands with a freer hand.[10] The Ottoman ruling elite, aware of the general weakening of its power, initiated extensive reforms of the administrative and military systems. But the degeneration of the Empire was deeper than the reach of these bureaucratic reforms; it was a general civilizational decline as well as a political and military one. Upon contact with Europeans, the Ottomans discovered that not only had they fallen woefully behind in military technology, but illiteracy and superstition plagued their subject peoples, and the institutions which were supposed to educate and inform were themselves in a state of disrepair.

Early Arab responses to the Ottoman decline took the form of religious and literary revivals with political overtones. One such response was the Wahhabi movement, begun by Muhammad bin Abdulwahhab in 1747. It called for a return to the original purity of Islam, which had been corrupted by superstition, innovations, and extraneous practices. One of Abdulwahhab's demands was a return to Arab leadership of the Islamic world. He found Muhammad Ibn Sa`ud, a chieftain from the Najd region, a powerful ally toward this end. It was not until the 1790s that the Wahhabis challenged the Ottoman caliphate outright by capturing the holy cities of Makkah and Madinah and threatening Baghdad and Damascus. They remained a threat until Egyptian governor Muhammad Ali, yielding to pressure from the Ottoman Sultan, sent a force to crush them in 1818. The Wahhabi movement had intellectual and cultural parallels in

Egypt and Iraq, and in cultural movements which began a critical study of *Hadith* (the body of traditions of the Prophet Muhammad), Arab history, and the Arabic language.[11]

The second challenge to the Ottoman sultan came from the same source which crushed the Wahhabi movement, Muhammad Ali. Ali, an Ottoman army officer of Albanian descent (ruled 1805–1848), not only established the *de facto* independence of Egypt from the Sultan, but extended his rule into Sudan and Syria. Ali's son, Ibrahim, governed Syria on his father's behalf. Although his rule lasted less than a decade (1833–1840), Ibrahim made a tremendous impact on that country. Among other things, Ibrahim established elementary schools in various parts of the country, improved the status of Christians, and allowed missionaries, especially American and French, to open their own schools. In addition, Ibrahim's rule contributed to the development of Arab national consciousness. A contemporary French envoy to the region relates that Ibrahim made no secret of his intention to restore Arab nationhood, to instill in the Arabs a real sense of patriotism, and to integrate them in the governance of the future empire.[12] Ibrahim's effort to establish an Arab empire failed in part due to British opposition to the project. The fact that Ibrahim himself was not an Arab did not help his cause. More seriously, the Syrians lacked a national consciousness at this stage. "The unifying force generated by the genius of the Prophet Muhammad has remained a force so long as Arab power had remained supreme," George Antonius writes. He continues:

> As that power waned, its cohesive influence weakened; the diverse peoples it had welded together into a cultural whole fell gradually asunder to form separate entities, regional and sectarian, according to the district or clan or creed to which they belonged. Side by side with that integration, a process of religious evolution was going on, which had led not only to the birth of new confessions, among both Moslems and Christians, but also to an increased emphasis on sectarian differences and to the growth of confessional loyalty as a substitute for cultural solidarity.[13]

The seeds of confessional loyalties which remain operative in the Fertile Crescent today were sown in this period, with expansion of the *millet* system into the Arab provinces. The *millet* system, developed by the Ottomans, granted some administrative autonomy to religious minorities. Confessionalism was strengthened by European powers which adopted one or another religious minority as proteges, as well as by the missionary schools. In the western part of the Arab world (the Maghreb) and the Arabian peninsula, where religious minorities either did not exist or were minuscule, tribalism played the same divisive role as confessionalism did elsewhere.

By the mid-nineteenth century, three major trends, not mutually exclusive but overlapping, prepared the ground for identity politics in the modern Arab world. These were Islamic revivalism, Arab nationalism or *qawmiyya*, and patriotism or *wataniyya.*

Qawmiyya

Arab nationalism began as literary revival. Syrian Christians, such as Butrus Bustani (1819–1893) with his dictionary *Muhit al-Muhit* and Nasif al-Yaziji (1800–1871) with his Arabic grammar aimed at youth, figured prominently in this movement. Another element in the literary revival was the wave of literary translation from European languages into Arabic, headed by Rifa`a al-Tahtawi (1801–1873), who in 1835 founded a translation institute in Egypt. "The Arab literary revival provided the logical base for the political revival. To them, language and the cultural heritage in which it is embedded, constituted the basis of national identity."[14] Language was a source of identity around which both Christian and Muslim could gather, and it is not surprising that its earliest and most eloquent advocates were Christian Arabs. "Awake ye Arabs and arise," Ibrahim al-Yaziji (1847–1906), Nasif's son, opened his famous poem which sang the glories of the Arabs and electrified both intellectuals and the masses with its ringing call to action. Note that, for the most part, *qawmiyya* defined itself against not European but Ottoman hegemony.

Arab nationalism did not necessarily mean separation from the Ottoman Empire. At first, *qawmiyya* simply meant an impassioned emphasis on the past achievements of the Arabs. Its proponents worked at creating a sense of Arab identity through the activities of literary and social clubs. Late in the nineteenth century, Arab nationalists began demanding more decentralization from Ottoman authority, even to the point of autonomy; still, the goal was improvement of the Arab provinces within the empire. Meanwhile, Turkish nationalism was growing, and the Young Turks' gains against Sultan Abdulhamid in 1908 advanced its progress. Arab nationalists initially welcomed the brother sentiment among the Turks, until it became obvious that their interests were at odds. Yet even at the First Arab Conference convened in Paris in 1913, most speakers called for decentralization and more Arab power in the central government, rather than independence. Some of these leaders returned home only to be executed by Jamal Pasha, Turkish governor of Syria. Even so, it took the pressure of the British, themselves motivated by the calculations of a cataclysmic World War, to move the Arabs to seek complete severance from the Ottoman Empire. In 1916, Sharif Hussein declared Arab independence and the Great Arab Revolt began.[15]

Neither was Arab nationalism exclusively secular, although its secular element, led by Christians and a few Muslims, was prominent. From the Christian point of view, the only viable political entity or organization would be based on the national rather than the religious principle of community. According to this view, a theocratic state like the Ottoman Empire was incompatible with "reason" and "progress" and contradicted the new consciousness of Arab identity.[16]

However, *qawmiyya* had an Islamic element too. For example, Abd al-Rahman al-Kawakibi (1849–1902), a Syrian Muslim intellectual, asserted the reciprocal relationship of Arab nationalism and Islam. He believed, echoing the Wahhabi movement a hundred years earlier, that Islam had given the Arabs political prominence and that Arab leadership was the key to reunifying the community of the faithful. He also decried despotism and considered the Ottoman Empire its prime example. The alternative to despotism was democratic government, and Kawakibi traced Arab traditions of democracy and deliberative consultation (*shura*) to the early period of Islamic history.[17] The Islamic component of Arab nationalism is also evident in Sharif Hussein's 1916 proclamation, in which he denounced the arbitrary tyranny of Jamal Pasha and the Young Turks as unIslamic, "represented the Arab revolt as a religious and national duty," and used his status as guardian of the holy city of Makkah to appeal for Islamic solidarity around his cause.[18]

Wataniyya

Patriotism, or love of the homeland, had roots in Arab heritage, but gained new meaning under Western influence, particularly the influence of the French Revolution. In Egypt, Rifa`a al-Tahtawi introduced the idea of the homeland as the object of sacrifice, and suggested that the brotherhood created by a common homeland, the *watan*, is equal to the brotherhood of faith. Islamic reformer Muhammad Abduh affirmed that the *watan* was the basis for political life and developed the notion of rights and obligations that bound the individual to the homeland.[19] In Syria, another alternative to sectarianism was *wataniyya* which was more locally derived than Arab nationalism. *Wataniyya* was an offshoot of nationalism but went one step further; it took as a basis of loyalty not the Arab nation as a whole but a specific locality or province. Thus when Egypt, Algeria, and Tunisia fell under European colonialism, *wataniyya* took the form, in each *watan* respectively, of Egyptian nationalism, Algerian nationalism, and Tunisian nationalism. While *qawmiyya* was directed mainly against the Ottoman Empire, *wataniyya* developed as a movement against European imperialism.

Islamic Revivalism

Three tiers can be distinguished in the Islamist trend: Individual intellectual reformers; the traditional Muslim masses; and organized Islamic groups. The writings of *ulama* like Jamal al-Din al-Afghani (1839–1897), Muhammad Abduh (1849–1905), Rashid Rida (1865–1935), and Shakib Arslan (1869–1945), raise a fundamental question: How can Muslims resist European hegemony and achieve strength without destroying their Islamic heritage and identity? Afghani, who was of Iranian origin but wrote in Arabic, espoused the unity of Islamic peoples and wanted to raise the Islamic consciousness of the masses. He believed that Muslim rulers acting in concert could resist Western hegemony, and initially supported the Ottoman sultan in an effort to realize this goal. Likewise, the Lebanese Arslan ardently supported the Ottoman state, out of a desire to see a powerful Islamic state to resist Europe. Syrian-born Rida, while he also advocated an Islamic state, rejected Ottomanism in favor of a Wahhabi-influenced approach to Islam's political dilemma. The journal he published in Egypt, *al-Manar*, had important impact in raising an Islamic consciousness among Arabs in the early twentieth century. From his exile in France, Abduh produced a journal addressing the problems of the Islamic world, with help from Afhgani. Abduh's goal was to remove the shackles of traditionalism, return to the original sources of Islam, and, through independent legal reasoning (*ijtihad*), develop Islamic thinking that could meet the challenges of modernity.

While thinkers like Afghani and Abduh had valuable insights for Islamic revivalism, the real power of this trend lay in the masses. "Ottomanism, Islamic reformism, and nationalism were the ideas of an educated urban minority . . . Beyond this minority . . . for the most part Islam as traditionally conceived still provided the motives which could urge men to action and the symbols in terms of which they gave it meaning."[20]

During the nineteenth century and until World War One, resistance to European occupation of Muslim lands came from religious movements and religious leaders. The Sanusiyya in Libya, the movement led by Abd al-Qadir in Algeria, and similar rebellions across North Africa, spoke the language of Islam and rallied the masses around Islamic symbols. The Sudanese Mahdiyya (1880–1899) was the most successful of these movements; its leader Muhammad Ahmad was able to displace the British-backed Egyptians and rule for nearly twenty years, drawing upon his Sufi education and his interpretation of Islamic sources.

The different solutions offered by thinkers and political movements in the Arab world of the late nineteenth and early twentieth centuries reflect not only disagreement over what was good for the Arab peoples, but also over conflicting approaches to identity. As one study of the period puts it, "disagreement ultimately lay in ambiguity regarding the nature of the national entity itself. Who are we? Muslims? Ottomans? Arabs? Egyptians? Christians?"[21]

While the Arab Revolt of 1916 was welcomed by many Arabs in the Fertile Crescent as an expression of Arab nationalism, the Revolt failed to bring independence for the area. Despite the promises given to Sharif Hussein by McMahon between 1915 and 1916,[22] the British government made a deal with France in 1916 to divide the area between them.[23] At the same time, the British government gave the leaders of the Zionist movement a promise to secure "the establishment in Palestine of a national home for the Jewish people."[24]

The First Arab Revolt ended in great disappointment for the majority of the inhabitants of the eastern Arab world. They witnessed the replacement of Ottoman rule with joint British and French military occupation under the name of a "mandate" given by the newly established League of Nations. Syria and Lebanon were placed under French mandate, while Iraq, Palestine, and Transjordan were under British rule. Thus by 1920, all the Arab countries except part of the Arabian peninsula came under European rule (see Maps 2.1 and 2.2). The ancient tie between the Arabs and the Turks ended with bitterness on both sides and was worsened by disputes over Turkish borders with Syria and Iraq.[25]

The Legacy of Colonialism

European colonial rule of the Arab world left a different legacy from one region to another. While the general goal of European control of the region was to secure sources of raw materials and markets for their products, some parts of the Arabian peninsula were controlled by Britain merely to secure a safe road to India. In the Gulf region, for example, Britain concluded treaties with the sheikhs of prominent tribes in order to use their lands as postal and provisional stations. Nonetheless, the colonial powers brought important changes to most Arab countries, including the introduction of financial, administrative, and communication reforms. Although these reforms appear to be positive, their main purpose was to maximize the exploitation of resources for the governments, companies, and individuals of the colonial powers.[26]

Although its dominance in the Arab world was short, European colonialism left a caustic legacy from which modern Arab nations are still recovering. The Arab world was colonized late in the history of Europe's imperialist project, at a time in which many Europeans were questioning the usefulness of that project. European imperialists of this era had there-

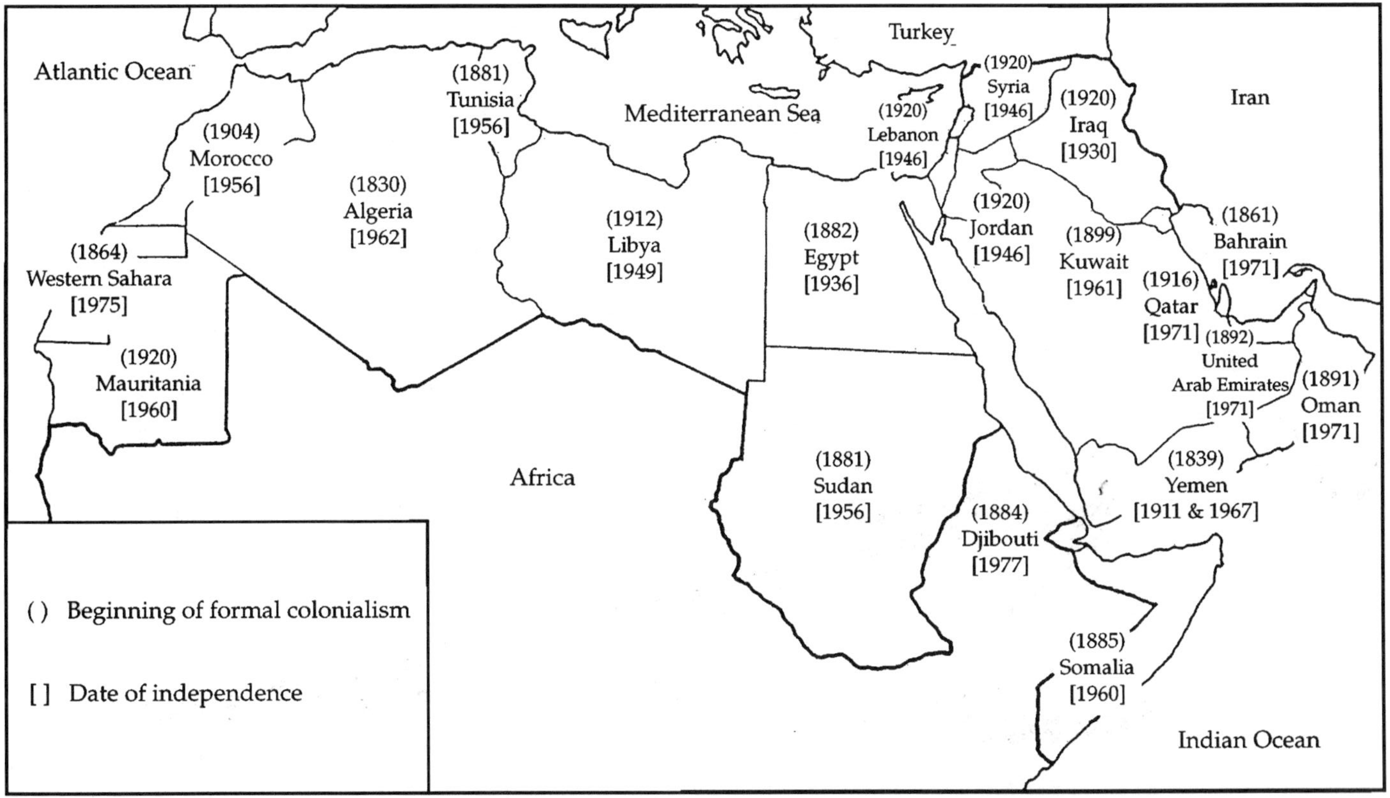

MAP 2.1 The Duration of European Colonial Rule over the Arab World. *Sources:* Some information for this map was compiled from *The Middle East and North Africa 1993*, 39th ed. (London: Europa Publications Ltd., 1992); and Rafic Boustani and Philippe Fargues, *The Atlas of the Arab World: Geopolitics and Society*, (New York, NY: Facts on File, 1991).

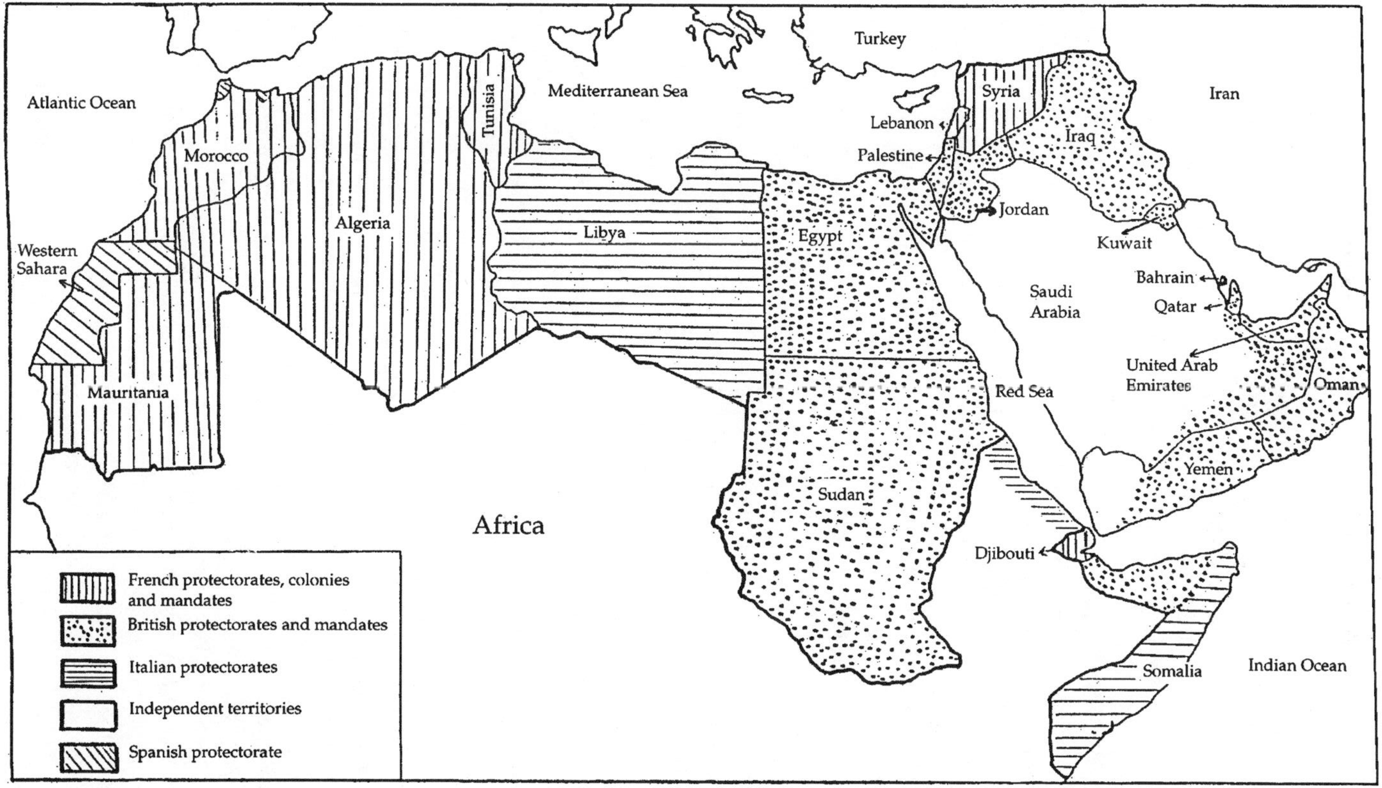

MAP 2.2 European Colonial Division of the Arab World, 1939. *Sources:* Some information for this map was compiled from *The Middle East and North Africa 1993*, 39th ed. (London: Europa Publications Ltd., 1992); and Rafic Boustani and Philippe Fargues, *The Atlas of the Arab World: Geopolitics and Society*, (New York, NY: Facts on File, 1991).

fore developed increasingly sophisticated and duplicitous rationalizations for colonization of the Arab world, calling it a "mandate" and claiming to be educating the colonized in self-government. Yet, to take one example of this rationalization, what the British described as a "temporary" occupation of Egypt lasted from 1882 till 1946 with little assistance in self-rule.[27] Such rationalization of colonialism perhaps damaged Arab identity-building more than straightforward domination might have done.

Regarding the Arab world's colonial legacy, four problems are especially salient.[28] The first is the rearrangement of the map which fragmented the Arab world into some twenty countries. In this context we can distinguish between three factors according to which colonial administrations redrew the boundaries of the region.[29] The first group of countries included those which had full or semi-independent status before European colonialism, including Morocco, Algeria, Tunisia, and Egypt. These countries' borders, despite their direct control by European powers, did not change much. The second group had not been subject to direct European control, yet their boundaries were drawn mainly by Britain. These countries include Saudi Arabia and the Arab Gulf states. The third group comprised countries created as a result either of the division of larger entities into smaller ones, or addition of territories. The Fertile Crescent region was divided to serve British and French interests. A drastic example of colonial administration radically remaking frontiers is the case of Greater Syria. Greater Syria was divided into four states: Syria, Lebanon, Jordan, and Palestine. The process began with France detaching the four areas of Ba`albek, the Beka`, Rasheyya, and Hasbayya, as well as the vilayet of Beirut and part of the district of Tripoli. These regions rich in agriculture were added to the Druze and Maronites' Mount Lebanon to satisfy the demands of the Maronite patriarchate. Second, France gave up the region of Mosul to Britain, exchanging it for an interest (25 percent) in the stock of the Turkish Petroleum Company. Finally, France granted the Sanjak of Alexandretta to Turkey (1939)—after nominal referendum—as a guarantee for Turkish neutrality in the coming war.[30] On the other hand, Iraq, Libya, Sudan and Mauritania were formed as a result of unification or addition of territories. For instance, Iraq came into existence in its current borders because of the addition of the three Ottoman vilayets of Mosul, Baghdad, and Basra. The redrawing of the Arab world left a heavy legacy of inter-Arab disputes, conflicts, and wars among neighbors. Without reducing the Iran-Iraq war and the Iraqi invasion of Kuwait entirely to border disputations, one can say that borders were an important issue in both these conflicts.

Another feature of the colonial period, the inability of the British government to reconcile its contradictory promises to Arabs and Jews in Palestine, laid the foundations of the most prolonged conflict in the region. While Israelis think of their struggle to establish a Jewish state in

Palestine as a liberation movement, Palestinians as well as other Arabs see the Jewish state as the worst type of imperialism, that is, settlement colonialism. The establishment of Israel uprooted at least a million Palestinians from their homeland, and those who remained were subjected to a total distortion of their Arabo-Islamic identity. The other Arab countries perceived Israel not only as the main obstacle to uniting the Asian and African sides of the Arab world, but also as an intrinsic threat to their existence because of its expansionist nature.[31] The British effort to establish a Jewish homeland created a bitter long term conflict that cost great human and material losses on all sides.

Thirdly, following the policies of "divide and rule," colonial powers encouraged ethnic and sectarian differences in the region. The European policy of selective intervention to protect one or another of the religious minorities started in the nineteenth century. The policies regarding the "Eastern Question" raised sectarian and confessional sensitivities between the Arab-Muslim majority and ethnic and religious minorities. The colonial powers, once in direct control, followed policies that would deepen hatreds between these groups. One example is French attempts to divide Arabs and Berbers by exempting the latter from subjection to *shari`a* in personal matters, replacing it with French laws in 1930, for the ostensible reason that Berbers were readier than Arabs to accept modernity.[32] Another example is the French reliance on the "Troupes Speciales" recruited from minorities, especially Alawites, to suppress resistance to colonial rule in Syria. Sectarian tensions that exist in Syria today cannot be adequately explained without examining the role of French colonial policy in nurturing them.[33]

The fourth gift of European colonialism was its distortion of socioeconomic development in the Arab world, as in most colonized lands. Colonial powers contributed to the creation of a modern sector in the economies of Arab countries: oil in the Gulf states, cotton in Egypt and Sudan, and phosphates in Morocco and Jordan. Most other sectors, meanwhile, were kept back. This helped elevate one segment of the population in wealth, education, and technological training, while maintaining the majority of the populace in underdeveloped conditions. The introduction of European laws in most Arab countries created a duality in the legal system: Islamic law was retained in personal matters (marriage, divorce, inheritance), while European codes were enforced in civic and economic life. After two to three decades of colonial rule, "two distorted economies, cultures, and societies" competed within the colonized lands.[34]

Local Nationalisms and Experiences of Representative Governments

The major types of political identity that dominated this period were those of *qawmiyya* and *wataniyya*. The nationalism of this period became more secular, taking the religious notion of *umma* but reformulating it in nationalist terms. While the idea of Arab nationalism did not wither away, the struggle for independence became the main concern of political movements. Consequently, Arab nationalism was reduced to the level of local submovements involved in the struggle against foreign rule.[35]

Nonetheless, most nationalist movements were not antagonistic to Islam. In fact, it was during this period that the leadership of the nationalist movements shifted from Christians to Muslims, albeit often to Muslims who were not very concerned with the question of Islamic identity. It was also during this period that many populist Islamic movements were founded; in particular, in 1928, the Society of the Muslim Brothers was established in Egypt by Hasan al-Banna.

The struggle for independence varied from peaceful resistance in the Gulf states and Lebanon to full scale armed struggle in Algeria and South Yemen, and a mix of political and military opposition in other countries. The first Arab country to gain formal independence was Egypt in 1920,[36] while Djibouti was the last in 1977. Most other Arab countries gained independence in the 1940s and 1950s.[37]

The newly independent Arab states had to cope with the problems of traditional society, the legacy of colonialism, and the challenges of nation-building. These challenges included building modern political institutions, developing the economy and the society, maintaining independence and strengthening loyalties to the new state, and containing social divisions.

Most Arab countries tried political systems with elected assemblies, similar to those of the colonial powers. The Arab countries which tried liberal or semiliberal democracies—Syria, Lebanon, Iraq, Egypt, Sudan, Somalia, Libya—did so before or immediately after independence. What is astonishing about the experiment is that in all these countries, representative government eventually ceased to exist. In fact, except in Lebanon, representative governments were replaced by authoritarian ones shortly after independence (see Table 2.1).

Why did the early experiments with representative government fail in virtually all Arab states? There are several reasons behind the failures. The first is that democratic elements, or apparently democratic elements, were introduced by the colonial power in each country in order to color its rule with some legitimacy. In most Arab countries such political systems emerged not through genuine choices by the population but through the will of the colonial administration. It follows that the exercise of semidemocracy was limited to satisfying the interests of the occupier. Despite the liberal tendencies among political elites in these countries, democracy was perceived by the majority of people as a euphemism for Western rule. Moreover, those elites that took part in and benefitted from

TABLE 2.1 Early Experiments with Representative Governments in Some Arab Countries

Country	*Date of Independence*	*Start of Representative Government Era*	*End of Representative Government Era*
Egypt	1936	1923	1952
Iraq*	1930	1921	1938
Jordan*	1946	1956	1957
Lebanon	1946	1926	1975
Libya	1951	1951	1969
Somalia	1960	1960	1969
Sudan*	1956	1956	1958
Syria*	1946	1928	1949

Note: *These countries also had subsequent experiences with democracy.

the limited political participation allowed in this period constituted less than ten percent of the total population.[38] The majority, in spite of frequent opportunities for voting, could not see the virtue or usefulness of this exercise. What was touted as "democracy" in the postindependence period preserved the egregious inequalities of the previous era and thus mainly served the interests of the traditional propertied classes. More or less the same elite families continued in their control of land and resources, but instead of traditional legitimation doctrines they now had a "modern" veneer and a democratic label. This holding pattern contributed to the hollowness of the postindependence "democratic" experiment for formerly colonized Arab peoples. Another factor made people perceive democracy unfavorably: The continuous splitting and subdivision of political parties into smaller groups, at a time when the need to create some kind of nation was foremost in people's minds.

The second reason behind the failure of the early democratic experiment was the first military defeat of the newly independent Arab nations in the war with the Zionist militia. In Egypt, Syria, and Iraq, the army officers who were to overthrow the postindependence "democratic civilian governments" were among those who suffered defeat in Palestine in 1948. These officers returned from the defeat demanding change, and vented their frustrations on the leaders sitting in their capitals by ousting them and installing military rule, thus ending the flirtation with democracy.[39]

Third, immediately following independence in the formerly colonized Arab countries, many segments of society were dissatisfied with the political systems and organized into political parties and social movements to work for change. The new movements spanned the ideological spectrum left to right, but all agreed on the obsolescence of liberal democracies and their inability to offer real answers to the major issues of the day. These movements presented an alternative to democracy. Their agenda included Arab unity, social justice, economic development, Islamic authenticity, and the liberation of Palestine. Moreover, these new groups came to draw their support from the lower and middle strata of society, in contrast to the higher classes who happened to control the "liberal" postindependence governments.

Since their prospects of gaining a piece of the pie by working from within the system were meager, the new movements questioned the basic legitimacy of the system and targeted liberal democracy. With the bitter experience of colonialism still fresh, it was no surprise that the post-independence generation of Arabs was disenchanted with the answers provided by the "liberal democracies" and was, by and large, attracted to these other alternatives. Some of these movements were influenced by communist ideologies, which appeared to be alternatives to liberal democracy in Europe as well. Among the alternative movements which became popular in the 1940s and 1950s were those "which would blend the elements of nationalism, religion, and social justice in a more appealing fashion. The Muslim Brothers were such a movement, particularly in Egypt, Sudan, and Syria. Communist and socialist groups also began to play a significant role in opposition both to imperial rule in its last phase and to the new governments which took its place."[40]

A combination of these three factors—which varied in degree from one Arab country to another—brought the early democratic experiments to an end. In most cases, it was the politicized army officers, through the popular movements, who brought down the early civilian, and to some extent elected, governments.[41] By the mid-1960s virtually all Arab countries, except Lebanon, were under the authoritarian rule of either populist republics or traditional monarchies.

The Authoritarian State and Pan-Arabism

There were four basic components in the ideologies of the populist republics: socialist domestic policies, Arab unity, standing up to Israel, and, at the level of international relations, identification with the "Third World" and neutrality in the Cold War. Ba`thism and Nasserism were the foremost ideologies of the populist type. Ba`thism emphasized the creation of one Arab state which would embody the Arab nation. Many of Ba'thism's founders came from religious minorities and secularism was an emphatic part of its ideology. The origins of Ba`thism "lay in intellectual debates about the national identity of the Syrians and their relations with other Arabic speaking communities; a debate which was more urgent in Syria than elsewhere, because the frontiers drawn by Britain and France in their own interests corresponded less than in most Middle Eastern countries to natural and historical divisions."[42]

Nasserism began as an enthusiasm for a charismatic figure and only later developed into an ideology. As an ideology, Nasserism contained the same bywords as Ba`thism—"Unity, freedom, socialism"—but in a different order: "Freedom, socialism, unity," with freedom defined first and foremost as the freedom of the nation (*watan*).[43]

Although some of the populist ideologies paid lip service to Islam, it was ancillary to the substance of their programs. Both Ba`thism and Nasserism institutionalized one-party rule during their time in power, which precluded the participation of the Islamist opposition in politics. The relationship of Nasser to political Islam, which began with his use of Islamic rhetoric,[44] soured quickly during his bitter clash with the Muslim Brotherhood, whose leaders he imprisoned and tortured. Ba`thism's and Nasserism's assignment of a tertiary role to Islam, and their fundamental underlying secularism, made the suppression of Islamists one feature of their respective terms in power.

Ba`thism and Nasserism became popular in the 1950s and early 1960s. Ba`thism was most popular as a movement; after it became the ruling ideology of Syrian and Iraqi regimes, its appeal waned. Nasser's early successes in nationalizing the Suez Canal and standing up to Britain, France, and Israel, ensured his popularity. However, after the secession of Syria from the UAR and Egypt's costly intervention in Yemen, disillusionment with Nasserism set in. Nasser's regime and those of the Ba`th in Syria and Iraq received their worst blow from the 1967 Arab defeat against Israel.

Democracy was not a priority in these and other populist socialist ideologies. A widespread conviction existed that democracy was a luxury which needed to be sacrificed for more important goals. Regimes which adopted these ideologies comprised part of a global trend in which many newly independent "Third World" countries drew strength from Eastern bloc models. These models were appealing because of their promise of fast economic development and because of their defiance toward the West, which still represented imperialism in the view of many people in the "Third World." In the so-called "progressive" regimes of the Arab world, democracy was criticized in socialist terms as a corrupt, inefficient Western ideology serving capitalist interests.

Democracy did not fare any better in the traditionalist conservative regimes, such as those of Saudi Arabia, Morocco, Jordan, and the Gulf states. Traditional rulers rejected democracy as a Western, "Christian" ideology alien to the "authentic" Arabo-Islamic heritage they claimed to represent. They characterized Western democracy as a decrepit, corrupt system which allowed undesirable, godless elements to rise and disrupt the public order.[45]

Such positions toward democracy were shaken by the 1967 Arab defeat and steadily undermined by the failures of Arab regimes to achieve any of the goals for which democracy was to be sacrificed. The legitimacy of both populist and traditionalist regimes was damaged in the 1970s by a growing realization that their lack of accountability may have been the cause of their failures. However, this damage was mitigated temporarily by the oil boom and the prosperity it brought. Mass dissatisfaction with regimes did not crystallize until oil prices collapsed in the early 1980s. Discontent at the economic hardships that hit most Arab households spilled over into political discontent. In addition to lower bread prices, protestors at demonstrations began demanding democracy. About this time, many regimes found it prudent to promote certain democratic openings in order to ease some of the discontent before it could reach a crisis point and threaten their hold on power. From this point on, democratization became the focus of attention of intellectuals, popular political movements, and Arab regimes themselves.

To sum up, the political identity of the Arab people until the nineteenth century had been one in which Islam was the frame of reference. Even Ottoman rule was acceptable to the Arabs as long as Islam remained the main source of identity because, in Islamic terms, the Ottoman sultan embodied the continuation of the Muslim caliphate. With the decrepitude of the Ottoman Empire in the face of increasing European domination, Arab awareness of a distinctly Arab political identity began to grow and to complicate the issue of collective identity with calls for Arab solidarity, Arab unity—Arab nationalism (*qawmiyya*). Western colonialism retarded the drive toward unity by carving the Arab world into twenty-some political entities. These subdivisions, although in most cases at odds with the historical character of the area divided, soon acquired a logic of their own. Independence from Western colonial administration meant independence in the form of the states created by that administration. These states became the basis of a new form of collective identity—*qutriyya*—and a history for these subdivisions was invented and projected backwards to produce a national mythology for this patriotism. In many of these states, freedom from Western imperialism came with calls for a return to the quest for Arab unity that had been delayed by colonization. This quest, including a solution to the Palestinian trauma; the postindependence goals of nation-building; economic development; and ongoing struggle against Western domination, became for a time the sacred ends for which the Arab peoples had to sacrifice democracy. Thus, the democratic moment just after independence was quickly swept aside by the urgency of what was, in fact, a fundamental disagreement over collective identity, the nature of the nation, and its priorities. Both kinds of regimes which ensconced themselves in the Arab world, populist republics and traditionalist monarchies, decided that democracy was to be forfeited in favor of other interests, such as modernization.

Late Ottoman rule, European domination, and postindependence *qutriyya* in the Arab world created the conditions for a crisis in collective identity. The crisis has two layers: the dispute over territorial borders and the dispute over what constitutes the ideological frame of reference for the postcolonial states. Together these form the basis of the conflict over collective identity. Arab nationalism and the Islamic movement are developments in this conflict, each with its (sometimes overlapping) centers of loyalty. This dynamic of conflict over collective identity, what Rustow calls the "hot family feud," continues to gum the gears of democratization.

The failure of the Arab regimes to achieve their much-touted goals and the declining welfare of Arab populations after the crash in oil prices in the early 1980s created mass disillusionment with the nationalist agenda and brought democracy to the forefront of popular demands. At the same time, Islamists were taking advantages of inroads opened by disenchantment with the older ideologies, whose inherent secularism had begun to look not only worn and tired, but suspiciously foreign and unauthentic as well. The appeal of political Islam increased and seemed to offer a new alternative in the debate over collective identity. The Islamist "solution" was also a reinvention of an old alternative, with just the shot of legitimacy lacking in the existing regimes. With widespread recognition of the arrival of Islamists in the arena, the question of Arab political identity entered a new phase.

Notes

1. Abd al-`Aziz al-Duri, *The Historical Formation of the Arab Nation*, trans. Lawrence I. Conrad (New York, NY: Croom Helm, 1987), p. 325.

2. Ibid., p. 29.

3. This does not mean "nation" in the specific sense of the nation-state which developed in Europe from the eighteenth century. I include the term "nation" with "community" in defining *umma* to convey a more distinctly political (as opposed to, say, cultural) basis of identity than that which "community" connotes. For the origin and development of the term nation, see, D. Rustow, "Nation," in David Sills, ed., *International Encyclopedia of the Social Sciences* (New York, NY: Macmillan/Free Press, 1969), Vol. 2, pp. 7–14.

4. Abd al-Rahman Sabuni, "Muhadarat fi Nizam al Hukm fil Islam" ("Lectures on the Political System in Islam"), unpublished papers, (United Arab Emirates: Shari`a and Law College, U.A.E. University, 1983), p. 26–34.

5. Termed "the Fertile Crescent" during a phase of European colonialism.

6. Albert Hourani, *The History of the Arab Peoples* (Cambridge, MA: Belknap Press of Harvard University, 1991), p. 5.

7. On political principles and systems in Islam, see Sabuni, "Muhadarat . . . ;" Muhammad S. El-Awa, *On the Political System of the Islamic State* (Indianapolis, IN: American Trust Publications, 1980); Muhammad Diya' al-Din al-Rayis, *al-Nazariyat al-Siyasiyya al-Islamiyya* (Islamic Political Theories), 3rd ed. (Cairo: Anglo-Egyptian Library, 1960).

8. Duri, *The Historical Formation of the Arab Nation*, p. 40.

9. Ibid., p. 103.

10. The European powers referred to their attempts to weaken and divide the Ottoman Empire in the late eighteenth and early nineteenth centuries as "the Eastern Question." On the origin of the Eastern Question, see L. Carl Brown, *International Politics and the Middle East* (Princeton, NJ: Princeton University Press, 1984), Part 1.

11. Duri, *The Historical Formation of the Arab Nation*, p. 141.

12. George Antonius, *The Arab Awakening* (New York, NY: Capricorn, 1945), p. 29.

13. Ibid, p. 32.

14. Hisham Sharabi, *Arab Intellectuals and the West: The Formative Years 1875–1914* (Baltimore, MD: Johns Hopkins, 1970), p. 115.

15. One of the best accounts of these events is that of Antonius.

16. Sharabi, *Arab Intellectuals and the West*, p. 18.

17. Abd al-Rahman al-Kawakibi, *Taba'i` al-istibdad wa masari` al- isti`bad* (The Characteristics of Tyranny and the Crimes of Oppression) (Cairo: n.p., n.d.).

18. For the Proclamation of the Arab Revolt, see Antonius, *The Arab Awakening*, chapter 10.

19. Duri, *The Historical Formation of the Arab Nation*, p. 157.

20. Hourani, *The History of the Arab Peoples*, p. 311.

21. Sharabi, *Arab Intellectuals and the West*, p. 106.

22. For the full text of the McMahon-Hussein correspondence, see Antonius, *The Arab Awakening*, "Appendix A."

23. The Anglo-Franco-Russian agreement generally known as the Sykes-Picot agreement.

24. The rest of the promise, known as the Balfour Declaration, asserted the will of Britain to facilitate this objective, without, however, prejudice or damage to "the civil and religious rights of existing non-Jewish communities in Palestine."

25. Hourani, *The History of the Arab Peoples*, p. 319.

26. Saad Eddin Ibrahim, *al-Mujtama` wal Dawla fil Watan al-`Arabi* (Society and State in the Arab World) (Lebanon: Markaz Dirasat al-Wahda al-`Arabia, 1988), p. 151.

27. Dankwart Rustow, "Arab Perceptions of History and the Question of Identity," in Stanley Renshon, ed., *The Political Psychology of the Gulf War: Leaders, Publics, and the Process of Conflict* (Pittsburgh, PA: University of Pittsburgh, 1993), p. 24.

28. An elaborate discussion of the legacy of colonialism can be found in Ibrahim, *Al-Mujtama` wal Dawla*, Chapter 3.

29. Adapted from Ibrahim, ibid.

30. Rafic Boustani and Philippe Fargues, *The Atlas of the Arab World* (New York, NY: Facts on File, 1991), p. 21.

31. Hence Israel is often described as a "dagger" in the heart of the Arab world.

32. Ibrahim, *Al-Mujtama` wal Dawla*, p. 159.

33. Another French divide-and-rule policy was to section the country into four mini-states: Damascus, Aleppo, an Alawite state, and a Druze state.

34. Ibrahim, *Al-Mujtama` wal Dawla*, p. 152.

35. Sharabi, *Arab Intellectuals and the West*, chapter 7.

36. There is disagreement over whether Egypt got independence in the 1920 Declaration or after the Treaty of 1936.

37. The exception is Saudi Arabia, which was never under European rule. However, the Saudi kingdom came into existence in its current borders in 1933 after a process of unification which had started in 1902.

38. Ibrahim, *Al-Mujtama` wal Dawla*, p. 192.

39. See Gamal Abd al-Nasser, *Egypt's Liberation: The Philosophy of the Revolution* (Washington DC: Public Affairs Press, 1955), for a marked expression of this.

40. Hourani, *the History of the Arab Peoples*, p. 403.

41. On the politicization of army officers see Patrick Seale, *The Struggle for Syria: A Study of Post-War Arab Politics*, (London: Oxford University Press, 1965).

42. Hourani, *The History of the Arab Peoples*, p. 404.

43. "Draft of the Charter of the United Arab Republic," in George Lenczowski, *The Political Awakening in the Middle East* (Englewood Cliffs, NJ: Prentice-Hall, 1970), p. 126.

44. See for example, *Egypt's Liberation: The Philosophy of the Revolution* (Washington, DC: Public Affairs Press, 1955).

45. Ghassan Salame, "Halat al-Ta`adudiyya al-Siyasiyya fil Mashriq al-`Arabi" (The Status of Political Pluralism in the Arab East) in Saad Eddin Ibrahim, ed., *al-Ta`adudiyya al-Siyasiyya wal Dimoqratiyya fil Watan al-`Arabi* (Political Pluralism and Democracy in the Arab World) (Amman: Muntada al-Fikr al-`Arabi, 1989), p. 145–6.

PART TWO

Democratization and Islamic Resurgence

3

Islamists and Democracy: The Intersection

Are the two trends, the push for democratization and the rise of Islamists, parallel or colliding popular forces in the Arab world? It seems that they developed side-by-side on separate tracks and are coincidentally simultaneous. The question of democratization has hovered over Arab political discourse at least since the era of the decolonization struggles, if not earlier. The concern for reintroducing Islam in the modern public realm also has a history dating back at least to the decline of the Ottoman Caliphate. It is not a coincidence, however, that in the 1980s and 1990s the Arab masses have pushed for more accountability for leaders, more participation in decision-making, and more democratization, while at the same time, larger and larger numbers of people have advocated an Islamic identity, Islamic authenticity, "Islamic solutions." Yet lately it seems as though democratization and Islamization may be colliding forces, or at least that Islamization seems to stop democratization dead in its tracks every time it gains momentum. This is not because of an essential incompatibility between the two as ideas; on the contrary, it is because they are so successful a couple that jealous regimes have kept them apart. Actually, they are neither parallel nor colliding, but rather overlapping processes whose conjunction contains the possibility of basic change in the collective identity of Arab polities. Every time a government begins to democratize, Islamists gain ground. At this infusion of Islam into the public realm, the government and segments of the society back away from democratization in alarm, questioning, "Is this who we are, who we want to be?"

That congealing of a sense of collective identity which, according to Rustow's model for transition to democracy, must begin to happen before people can come together as a democratic polity, is still in its early stages in many Arab countries today. Yet collective identity is not a discrete goal to be achieved but a dynamic, and that dynamic is certainly alive in today's Arab world. The contours of the debate over collective identity have shifted. In the 1950s and 1960s, the debate did not seriously or centrally include Islamic identity as an alternative or a cluster of alternatives; in the 1980s and 1990s, it does. I will detail how the two processes, democratization and the rise of Islamists, have emerged in the Arab world.

Democratization Measures Since the Mid-1980s

In a survey of democratization trends since 1985, three patterns or issues emerge. To begin with, the first year of the 1990s brought many indications of democratization. Even the most despotic regimes were pressured to adopt at least cosmetic measures in that direction. Both Syria and Iraq conducted parliamentary elections that year, in which more independents were allowed to enter the parliaments (see Table 3.1). Following that year, traditional monarchies in two oil states, Bahrain and Oman, felt obliged to appoint a "consultative council," and a third, Saudi Arabia, inaugurated its sixty-member consultative council. Secondly, in countries which took more serious steps toward democracy, including Tunisia, Algeria, Egypt, Jordan, and Yemen, further democratization has yet to happen. To make a further distinction within this group, Jordan and Yemen made progress toward the possibility of further democratization, while the other three suffered reversals. Third, rather than taking one criterion, such as the lack of a peaceful transfer of power, and arriving at a blanket conclusion that covers all the countries surveyed, we must make distinctions along a continuum from most repressive to most democratically open.

Human rights are one of the criteria used to measure democracy, since basic civil liberties are required if people are to be part of the political decision-making process and to hold rulers accountable. It is very difficult to make generalizations about human rights violations because there have been fluctuations yearly. For example, Tunisia improved its human rights record between 1987 and 1989, but deteriorated in this regard after its confrontation with Islamists in 1989. The human rights violations of two other countries, Egypt and Algeria, in the form of detentions, executions, and violent raids on suspected terrorists, have steadily escalated to unprecedented levels during the 1990s. Following the cancellation of the second round of parliamentary elections in January 1992, Algerian authorities arrested thousands of FIS members and sympathizers. In protest, Islamists began a violent campaign against the regime. Between January 1992 and December 1995, there were over 50,000 victims of violent acts committed by governmental forces and Islamist protestors.[1] In Egypt, a record-breaking sixty executions have occurred under Mubarak; 660 people died and over 1000 were wounded by political violence from January 1992 to November 1994.[2] In both countries, amendments to antiterrorism laws have raised concerns because they give governments sweeping powers to detain people.

TABLE 3.1 Indications of Democratization in Some Arab States Between 1985 and 1990

Country	*Year*	*Indications*
Algeria	1989	Ruling party ends monopoly over power and allows political pluralism
	1990	Free local and regional elections
Egypt	1987	Parlimentary election. There are functioning opposition & freedom of speech
	1990	Court rules that the composition of the 1987 elections was unconstitutional
Iraq	1989	Committee set up to draft new constitution
		Elections to the National Assembly brought in more Independents
Jordan	1989	Free parliamentary election
	1990	Travel restrictions on opposition lifted; *Mukhabarat* power reduced; etc.
Libya	1988	All political prisoners allegedly released
Sudan	1986	Free parliamentary election after Numayri's dictatorship overthrown
Syria	1990	Elections for People's Council—number of Independents allegedly increased
Tunisia	1987	President Bourguiba overthrown
	1989	Parliamentary election, but ruling party won all seats
	1990	Opposition participating in committee to amend electoral law
Yemen	1988	First general election for Consultation Council

Source: Compiled from data in *Keesing's Record of World Events*, Vols. 30–36, 1986–1990.

On the positive side, human rights organizations have been established in both Yemen and Kuwait. A Freedom House survey changed the categorization of three Arab nations, Kuwait, Oman, and the United Arab Emirates, from nonfree to partially free countries. Jordan, Lebanon, and Yemen improved their ratings. The overall record, however, is still grim. As of early 1993, no Arab country is totally free according to Freedom House's criteria; only ten Arab countries are partly free states, and the rest are nonfree states.[3]

Survey of Democratizing Measures

An overview of democratizing steps, such as free elections and human rights improvements, shows that most Arab states still fall short. As Table

3.2 shows, only five out of 21 countries have had free elections since 1985: Sudan in 1986; Jordan in 1989 and 1993; Algeria in 1990 and 1991; Kuwait in 1992; and Yemen in 1993. There was only one peaceful transfer of power: Sudan in 1986. Following the tables is a country-by-country examination of democratization measures.

1. At the repressive extreme stand Syria, Iraq, and Libya. Regimes in these states do not grant opposition parties legal status. Only token parties allied with the ruling elites officially exist in Syria and Iraq, while partisanship is entirely banned in Libya. Presidential elections are uncontested, unsupervised by any nonregime organization, and usually garner 99.99 percent of the vote for the incumbent. (This is the figure yielded by the 1991 plebiscite for seven more years of Asad, for example.)

2. At the other end of the continuum are Jordan, Yemen, and pre-1992 Algeria. Both the 1989 Jordanian parliamentary elections and the 1990 Algerian local elections were important because most major political forces participated, because the opposition won more than half the vote, and because the elections were accompanied by other moves toward democratic opening. In Algeria, the election was one result of a chain of political and economic reforms which included the end of one-party monopoly of power and the establishment of a multiparty system.

In Jordan, emergency law regulations in effect since 1967 were frozen; the powers of the Extraordinary Courts and the *Mukhabarat* (secret police) were reduced; some political prisoners were released; and passports confiscated to prevent regime opponents from travelling abroad were returned. Legislation passed in 1992 permitted the formation of political parties, and in late December parties were allowed to issue their own newspapers for the first time in forty years.[4] By late 1993, there were twenty political parties, representing a wide spectrum from communist to Islamist and from liberal to conservative.

What puts Yemen in this category as well is the April 1993 parliamentary elections, the first since unification of North and South Yemen. A multiparty system without restrictions had been launched a year before, and an extraordinary 46 parties responded by registering. Neither of the two ruling parties, the People's Congress and the Socialist Party, won a majority in the elections, which were under voluntary international supervision. While the two ruling parties were able to work together for almost three years, a political crisis erupted in the summer of 1993. The essence of the crisis was disagreement over power-sharing between the General People's Congress and the Yemeni Socialist Party, which threatened the unity between the North and the South. Mediation efforts were launched by Jordanian, Egyptian and Omani officials to prevent the crisis from exploding. In February 1994 the leaders of the two parties signed

TABLE 3.2 Survey of Elections in Arab Countries: 1985–1995

Country	*Elections*	*Free or Not*	*Power Transfer*
Algeria	Local '90	Yes	No
	Parliament '91	Yes*	No
	Presidential '95	Yes	No
Egypt	Parliament '87	No	No
	Shura '89	No	No
	Parliament '90	No	No
	Presidential '93**	No	No
	Parliament '95	No	No
Iraq	Parliament '89	No	No
	Presidential '95**	No	No
Jordan	Parliament '89	Yes	No
	Parliament '93	Yes	No
Kuwait	Council '90	No	No
	Parliament '92	Yes	No
Lebanon	Parliament '93	No	No
Mauritania	Local '90	n.d.***	No
	Presidential '92	n.d.***	No
	Parliament '92	n.d.***	No
Morocco	Parliament '93	n.d.***	No
Sudan	Parliament '86	Yes	Yes '86
Syria	Parliament '90	No	No
	Presidential '91**	No	No
Tunisia	Parliament '89	No	No
	Presidential '94**	No	No
N. Yemen	Parliament '88	Yes	No
Yemen	Parliament '93	Yes	No

Notes: *The second round of the election was canceled.
**These were one-candidate referenda on the incumbent president.
***No data.
Sources: *Keesing's Record of World Events,* Vol. 31–41, 1985–1995; *The Middle East and North Africa 1993,* 39th ed. (London: Europa Publications Ltd., 1992); *Civil Society,* Vols. 1–3, 1992–1994.

a document in which they pledge to resolve their dispute peacefully, yet both sides were mobilizing their armed forces even at the time of the signing. In May the tension between the two sides escalated into a full-scale civil war. Leaders of former South Yemen announced the formation of a new state, the Democratic Republic of Yemen. In July, the Northern forces of President Ali Abdullah Saleh were able to inflict a crushing defeat on the separatists, bringing an end to two months of civil war and preserving the unity of Yemen, after 7,000 deaths, 15,000 wounded, and three billion dollars of damage to the country. In a letter to the UN Secretary-General, the leaders of the victorious side pledged to declare full and comprehensive amnesty for the separatists, to carry out relief efforts, to respect democracy, pluralism, and human rights, and to resume national dialogue in the framework of constitutional legitimacy.[5]

Since the military coup in Algeria and the interruption of Yemen's democratization by civil war, Jordan remains in 1994 the only Arab country to cautiously continue its experiment with democratization. Yemen's constitution is being revised and an amendment to limit presidential terms was adopted after Saleh was re-elected. This and the fact that the southern-based Socialist Party was not banned after the war but continues its activities within a multiparty framework, are signs of strong possibility for further democratization in Yemen. Whether there will be a real transfer of power in the next presidential and parliamentary elections will be the test.

3. The six Gulf states constitute another cluster in the middle of the continuum. Kuwait stands apart here as the only Gulf country to hold elections for parliament and officially to allow opposition parties to contest seats in its National Assembly. The 1992 parliamentary election was significant because oppositional Islamists won more than half the seats.

4. Sudan and Algeria are countries which took great strides toward democracy but reached an impasse that was resolved by military coup.

5. Tunisia and Egypt have swerved unevenly between democratizing measures and repressive measures. In March 1994, Tunisia held presidential and parliamentary elections. President Ben Ali won the usual 99.9 percent of the vote. His party won 144 of 163 seats in Parliament. Three other parties were allowed to win the remaining nineteen seats based upon 2.27 percent of the popular vote. By comparison, in 1989, candidates sympathetic to the Islamist Nahda party had won (according to the government calculations) 14 percent of the popular vote but, on a technicality, were not allowed to get seats. In another indication of the regime's faint commitment to democratization, human rights activist Munsif Marzuqi and oppositional party leader Abd al-Rahman al-Hani were arrested for declaring their intention to run for president against Ben Ali.[6]

6. In Morocco and Mauritania there have been several elections with relatively fair procedures. Morocco had a parliamentary election in 1993. Political parties which already had legal recognition were allowed relatively free contestation in the election, but Islamist parties were not recognized and restrictions were placed on their activities. Since 1990, Mauritania has seen local, presidential, and parliamentary elections. The local elections were held in December 1990. Voters had a choice between four rival lists compiled by the government. In the capital, it was reported that Islamists won two-thirds of the seats.[7] The country's first presidential

elections were held in January 1992, and resulted in the re-election of President Colonel Moaouia Ould Taya. Rather than the 99.9 percent typical for presidential returns in Arab states, Taya won only 62.7 percent of the vote, which is a good indication. His main challenger, Ahmed Ould Daddah, came second with 32.7 percent. Elections for the National Assembly were held in March and resulted in victory for the Social Democratic Republican Party, the party affiliated with the president. Out of the total 79 seats, the SDRP won 67 seats. Two other parties won one seat each, and the remaining 10 seats went to Independent candidates. The major limitation of this election was the fact that the polls were boycotted by six oppositional groups, including the Union of Democratic Forces, the leading oppositional party.[8]

7. Lebanon, on the other hand, with its long denominational democratic tradition, seems to have regained some of its political health and held parliamentary elections in September 1992. While most political forces among Maronite Christians boycotted this elections, it was significant because it incorporated into the political process groups such as Amal, Hizbullah, and Sunni Islamists, for the first time. "The showing of Islamic forces, Shi`i and Sunni alike, was striking and reflected, in significant measure, an impressive campaign to build political support at the grass roots. . . . Lebanon's democracy may be back on track."[9] Lebanese political life, including any prospect for further democratization, is strained, however, by the presence of Syrian armed forces on its soil and the constant intervention of other external powers such as Israel.

8. Somalia is a lone case of disintegration into civil conflict, although international effort has been made to stop further deterioration.

Explaining Democratization

What led up to the democratic opening just described? Despite the difficulty of generalizing about all these countries, there are several common factors. Ruling elites faced multiple pressures. These include tremendous socioeconomic problems as a result of the increase in population and urbanization over the last two decades. Coupled with higher levels of education, this means that regimes face a populace with new demands and higher expectations. As oil prices decreased and import substitutions steadily rose, by the mid-1980s many Arab countries were not able to subsidize basic commodities, provide services, and create jobs. Many Arab countries witnessed debt crises which led them, on the recommendation of the International Monetary Fund, to raise food prices. These measures provoked mass rioting in a number of countries: first Egypt in 1977, then Morocco, Sudan, Tunisia, followed by Algeria and Jordan in 1988 and 1989 respectively. In the Jordanian case, demonstrators demanded, in addition to cancellation of the price increases, the resignation of the unpopular government of Zaid Rifa`i. In Algeria, the confrontation between demonstrators and police produced hundreds of casualties. In both countries, the leadership decided that these economic shocks required some kind of political liberalization. Arab countries seem to fit what Rustow describes as a catch-22: "If the economy declines under heavy burdens of rising prices, unemployment or foreign debt, the rulers will face growing opposition or violent unrest. If the economy expands with a thriving middle class and growing export sector, pressure mounts for political liberalization and change of regime."[10]

Second, civil society has grown. In many Arab countries, opposition groups, including Islamic movements, were founded independently of the state. With the failure of the state to provide essential services and meet the basic needs of the population, some of these groups stepped in to fill the gap. This was especially apparent when natural disasters hit the region, such as the earthquakes in Egypt and Algeria. It was Islamist groups which led relief efforts to victims. Therefore, ruling elites in some countries concluded that it would be better to contain such groups within the system, which meant taking some democratizing measures.

The third factor is less tangible. It is a shift in sensibilities: Classes which had been persuaded to sacrifice political freedom for the sake of ideals such as social justice, anti-imperialism, and Arab nationalism were disillusioned with the results of this trade-off. Such slogans no longer appealed to the middle and working classes which had emerged since independence.[11] Among Arab intellectuals, the new vocabulary began to emphasize pluralism, freedom, and democracy.

A fourth pressure was the demonstrative effect of the changes in East Europe and other parts of the world in the late 1980s. Changes in East Europe encouraged the democratization impulse in the Arab world. Millions of Arabs watched the fall of the Berlin Wall and the bloody overthrow of Nicolae Ceaucescu. Rustow argues that the strongest pressure for change is created by intensified global communication. News sources reported that Eastern Europe's heady changes inspired the opposition movement in preinvasion Kuwait to call for the restoration of parliament, made people in Jordan and Algeria more adamant in their demand for real change, and helped the press in some Arab countries to openly denounce corruption and abuse of power.[12] Moreover, democratic opening in one Arab country had an affect on surrounding countries. For example, Syrians could follow the exciting restoration of Jordan's parliament on Jordanian television, and Arabs everywhere watched the hesitant steps toward democracy in Algeria with great concern bordering on euphoria.

All these pressures combined forced ruling elites to realize that they had to liberalize their regimes to survive. Precisely because liberalization was a survival tactic for them, the point at which regimes realized that liberalization was going to lead to their demise was the moment they decided to reverse it. The decision to reverse liberalization was hastened by early evidence that it was bringing Islamist opposition dangerously close to power.

The early 1990s revealed that these two trends, popular Islamization and democratization, had been developing simultaneously. What was their relationship to each other?

Islamist Advances

Islamists have been able to win ground in almost every election that had some degree of fairness and freedom. The following section is a survey of elections since the mid-1980s and how Islamists fared in them.

Egypt

The first general election in which Islamists won seats was the parliamentary election of 1984. Despite the restrictive electoral law requiring parties to gain a minimum of 8 percent of the total vote in order to be represented, and despite alleged fraud,[13] the New Wafd Party, which had just allied with the Muslim Brotherhood, won 59 seats (15.8 percent). The ruling National Democratic Party won 72.9 percent. The Muslim Brotherhood entered the alliance because they would not have been able to run on their own, not being recognized as a legal party. Islamists won eight of the alliance's combined 59 seats. The significance of this election is that it was the first in more than thirty years to include opposition candidates. In addition, the New Wafd was the only opposition party, with its Islamist allies, to cross the 8 percent threshold.

Several factors combined to set the stage for a freer election of the People's Assembly in 1987. Demonstrations staged by Islamists to protest Asyut University's ban against women who wanted to cover their faces on campus constituted one factor. Another was an attempted coup by officers linked to Islamic Jihad.[14] Moreover, Mubarak wanted to secure a second term as president by proving himself a real democrat. Early in 1987, Mubarak's government called for a referendum to hold early elections and amend the electoral law, providing 48 seats for independent candidates. The elections, however, maintained the dominance of the ruling National Democratic Party, which gained 346 seats, compared with 389 in 1984. Having proved themselves strong partners, the Muslim Brotherhood became a desirable ally. They joined with both the Socialist Labor Party and the Liberal Social Party to form the Islamic Alliance, which won a combined total of 60 seats, of which the Bro hood's share was 37, making it the largest single opposition group in the Assembly. The New Wafd won only 35 seats. Thus not only had the opposition scored the largest number of seats (95 plus 7 independents) since Nasser's takeover, but Islamists—both the Brotherhood and their allies—had made steady advances and become the official opposition to the ruling NDP.

The opposition parties ran in the elections for the Shura Council (the upper house) in 1990 and did not win any seats, accusing the government of widespread fraud and intimidation.[15] Having lost faith in the government's honesty, and to protest the government's refusal to allow judicial monitoring of the election, the major opposition parties, including the New Wafd and the Islamic Alliance, decided to boycott the 1990 elections for the People's Assembly.[16]

In November and December 1995, parliamentary elections were held. Scores of Islamist candidates were harassed, arrested, put on trial and sentenced "to jail terms of three or more years for their involvement in nonviolent political activities" shortly before the campaign period.[17] In just one day early in the campaign period, three hundred Islamist campaign workers and observers were imprisoned.[18] Over the course of the elections, close to a thousand Islamists were arrested. One Islamist gained a seat as an Independent. The ruling party garnered 93.6 percent of the seats in one of the most fraudulent elections conducted during Mubarak's reign.

Sudan

Sudan's most significant free election took place in 1986, after the popular uprising of 1985 brought down the military regime of Ja'far al-Numayri. More than 40 political parties contested for seats in parliament during April 1986. The two traditional parties, Ummah and the Democratic Unionists, won the largest number of seats, 99 and 63 respectively. The Islamists, represented by the newly formed National Islamic Front (NIF), came in third with 51 seats. Although Islamists ranked third after the two traditional parties, they had made tremendous advances in two respects. First, their numbers had increased dramatically from the previous election before military rule, in which they had only won three seats. Second, they dominated the "constituency of the graduates," and came first among the educated sectors in major cities.[19]

On June 30, 1989, a military coup placed General Omar Hasan al-Bashir in power in Sudan. After an initial period of confusion, it became clear that the new regime favored the National Islamist Front and that these Islamists enjoyed influence in its ranks. This makes Sudan the only country in the Arab world where Islamists have state power, and all eyes are upon it. The regime has promised to hold parliamentary and presidential elections, having held local elections in 1992–1993. However, organizing on the basis of political parties is banned. So far, the regime seems to be prioritizing the war in the South, social order, and economic self-sufficiency at the expense of democratic practice. Its Islamist orientation has put the state at odds with the West and many of the Arab regimes, making it the topic of a great deal of misinformation, so that it is difficult to sort out the facts. The new government has not shown enough commitment to democracy to satisfy its critics. Other Islamists are looking to Sudan to provide a model. If Sudan is a model, it is a model for the transition to power by military rather than democratic means. Given the roadblocks in the path of Islamists' democratic ascension to power (e.g. Algeria), this seems to some Islamists to be an appropriate response to hypocritical democratic posturing by established regimes which have no intention of allowing Islamists meaningful participation even when they follow all the rules.

Kuwait

In the 1985 National Assembly Elections, Islamists (Muslim Brotherhood, Salafi, and Shi`i) won several of the total 50 seats. While no political parties were officially recognized, Islamists did better than the Arab nationalists (five seats) and came after the traditional and mostly "independent" candidates who tend to support the government.

In the first election after the Iraqi invasion, held in October 1992, oppositional forces won a majority of almost 35 seats. Of these, 19 belong to Islamist groups, 16 are identified with secular democratic groups, and the remaining 15 are regarded as progovernment or royalist.[20]

Lebanon

Both Shi`i and Sunni Islamist groups gained ground in contesting for the 60 parliamentary seats designated for Muslims in the first elections there in almost twenty years, which was held in September 1992. According to news reports, Hizbullah's candidates won twelve seats and Sunni Islamists won at least five seats. Islamist victories in parliament on such a scale reflect a rise in the popularity of Islamist groups among the Muslim population.

Tunisia

The first election for parliament since Ben Ali ousted former president Bourguiba took place in February 1989. Although the government did not permit Islamists to participate as a legal political party, Islamists contested in the election, presenting candidates in 19 out of the 25 constituencies. While the ruling party, the RCD, won all the 141 seats, Islamist candidates won 14 percent of the vote nationwide and a stunning 30 percent in major cities like Tunis and Sousse.[21] Opposition candidates, particularly Islamists, accused the government of widespread electoral fraud. According to Rashid al-Ghannouchi, the leader of the Islamist party Al-Nahda, Islamists won between 50–80 percent of the vote, especially in major cities, and the government candidates did not get more than 20 percent. The government was alarmed by the results and decided to lean more toward suppression, Ghannouchi maintains.[22] Islamists were totally excluded from the 1994 parliamentary election; the major Islamic movement, al-Nahda, was outlawed and harshly suppressed by the security forces.

Yemen

There was an important election for the consultative council in the Yemen Arab Republic in July 1988, before unification with South Yemen. Over half the elective seats went to the Muslim Brotherhood and its sympathizers.[23] Islamists maintained their strong presence in the first election for the 301-member parliament after the unification of the two Yemens. The Islamists, renaming their party al-Islah, came second with 62 seats. The General People's Congress Party, which had ruled North Yemen before unification, won 131 seats, and the party which had ruled South Yemen came in third with 56 seats. Several smaller parties won the remaining seats (see Table 3.3).

The major Islamic party, the Yemeni Alliance for Reform (Islah), sided with the Northern forces in the civil war, which ended with victory for them. Because of their active role in the war, Islamists have advanced on two grounds. First, they joined the People's Congress Party to form the first government after the end of the war, taking nine portfolios out of the 28 total. Second, Islamists were able to pass an amendment to the Constitution making Islamic law *(shari`a)* "the source of all legislation."

Jordan

There have been two parliamentary elections since the 1988 riots protesting price hikes on basic commodities and demanding the resignation of the government. The first election was held in November 1989, with 647 candidates, most of whom were independent, due to a ban on political parties. The Muslim Brotherhood candidates were the winners, gaining 22 of the total 80 seats. If we add to this number the 12–17 seats of other

TABLE 3.3 1993 Parliamentary Election Results in Yemen

Party	*Seats*
General People's Congress	121
Yemeni Alliance for Reform (Al-Islah)	62
Yemeni Socialist Party	56
Arab Socialist Ba`th Party	7
Truth Party	2
Nasserite Popular Unionist Organization	1
Nasserite Correction Organization	1
United Democratic Front	1
Independent	47
Undeclared	3
Total number of seats	301

Source: Keesing's Record of World Events, Vol. 39, No. 4, 1993, p. 39440.

independent Islamists, the Islamist bloc formed approximately one-half of the parliament. In the second election, in November 1993, the Islamist bloc shrank to 22 seats. The newly established Islamic Action Front, dominated by the Muslim Brotherhood, won only 18 seats, while independent Islamists won four seats. Although this setback is significant, it does not reflect a major loss in popularity for at least two reasons. First, Islamists remain the largest organized bloc in the new parliament. Second, they won almost 30.5 percent of the popular vote.[24]

Algeria

The first free elections which followed the liberalization measures in Algeria were the local and regional elections of 1990. The newly formed Islamic Salvation Front (known by its French acronym FIS) won a massive victory of 853 out of 1539 local councils (55.4 percent) and 32 of the *wilayahs* (regions or states) (see Table 3.4).

The Algerian local election was not a mere propaganda ritual but a manifestation of significant change because (1) election procedures were free and fair; (2) the opposition, especially Islamists, won more than half the vote despite the desires of Algeria's rulers; and (3) the election was accompanied by other important moves of political and economic reforms, including the end of one-party monopoly of power and the establishment of political pluralism.

No wonder it was widely believed that Algeria after the local elections "emerged as the most liberal political system in the Arab world."[25] However, many observers of Algeria predicted that the Islamists would not do

TABLE 3.4 1990 Algerian Local and Regional Election Results

Affiliation	*Local*	*Percent*	*Regional*	*Percent*
Islamic Salvation Front	853	55.4	32	66.6
National Liberation Front (ruling party)	487	31.6	14	29.3
Rally for Culture & Democracy	87	5.6	1	2.08
Independents	106	6.8	1	2.08
Algerian Innovation Party	2	0.3	0	0
National Party for Consolidation & Development	2	0.3	0	0
Social Democratic Party	2	0.3	0	0
Totals	1,539	100	48	100

Sources: Al-Islah, No. 146, July 1990, p. 12; *New York Times,* July 14, 1990.

as well in the subsequent parliamentary election, attributing the initial Islamist victory in large part to the abstention of two major secular parties, the Front for Socialist Forces (FFS) and the Algerian Democratic Movement (MDA). To the disappointment of these analysts, in the first round of the first free multiparty elections for parliament in December 1991, the Islamist Salvation Front won 188 seats in the 430-member legislature. The Front for Socialist Forces was a distant second with 25 seats, and the ruling National Liberation Front had only 15 seats. With the FIS expected to win at least 150 of the 199 seats still to be decided in the second round, the Algerian army forced President Chadli Benjedid to resign on January 11 and pressured the prime minister into canceling the elections the next day. The government arrested prominent FIS leaders, a move followed by protests and demonstrations throughout the country. On March 4, 1992, the government banned the FIS.[26]

Since then, Algeria has witnessed a full-scale civil war in which tens of thousands have been killed. The governing junta has come to realize that they cannot turn back the clock and roll back the democratization process entirely. On November 16 1995, the regime organized the first multiparty presidential election since Algeria's independence. The incumbent, Liamine Zeroual, took 61.34 percent of the vote, emerging victorious against three other candidates. The three candidates represented Hamas, a moderate Islamist party; the liberal Party for Alergian Renewal (PRA); and the Rally for Culture and Democracy (RCD), a secular Berber nationalist party. This presidential election was important for several reasons. First, turnout was as high as 75 percent. Voters saw the elections as a way of ending the civil strife and returning to the democratic route. Second, an Islamist candidate was allowed to run. The Islamist, Mahfoud al-Nahnah, came in second at 25.3 percent of the vote—still a significant vote of confidence for moderate Islamists, as opposed to the extremist Armed Islamic Group (GIA), which boycotted the election. The president allowed genuine contestation for his office by bona fide opponents. Third, in a climate where most presidents garner at least 99 percent of the vote in any election (e.g. Syria's Asad got 99.82 in 1991; Egypt's Mubarak, 94.0 in 1993; Tunisia's Ben Ali, 99.91 in 1994; and who could forget Saddam's 99.47 in 1995), the incumbent's acknowledgement of his 61.34 returns indicated a new disposition in Arab politics. Like Mauritania's 1992 presidential election in which incumbent Taya accepted a modest 62.7 percent, this result ushers in an era of rulers who are slightly more concerned with their credibility among the masses.

The FIS victory in 1991 was a turning point for both ruling elites and the masses in the Arab world. It provided additional proof of the mass disenchantment with the ruling elites and left no doubt in the mind of rulers who would win if they were to allow free elections to take their course. It jolted the debate over collective identity with a surge of energy from a new, contending discourse—Islamist discourse. But as Islamists were making headway toward power through freely contested elections, many ruling elites were working to contain and co-opt this threat before it was too late. The Algerian coup and resulting civil war showed that reversing democratization is terribly costly. The subsequent presidential election was the action of a subdued regime which had learned the lesson that rule without a mandate from the people was no longer possible in Algeria, and that it was no longer tenable to exclude all Islamists from politics.

How much of a threat do the Islamists really pose? Are the ruling elite and other secular forces justified in their perception of the Islamist threat? I will address these questions in the following section by examining what constitutes the Islamist challenge: Who are the Islamists and how do they enter the picture of the contemporary Arab world? What are their ideological agendas and what are their positions toward democracy?

Notes

1. This figure is based on both official and oppositional estimates, and it includes Islamists, security forces, and innocent civilians.

2. *New York Times*, Dec. 4, 1994, p. 6; *Civil Society*, Jan. 1994, p. 30 and Nov. 1994, p. 7.

3. *Freedom Review*, Vol. 24, No. 1, 1993.

4. *Middle East International*, Dec. 1 and 17, 1989; *Keesing's Record of World Events*, Vol. 39, p. R139, Nov. 1993.
5. *Keesing's Record of World Events*, Vol. 40, No. 7–8, 1994, p. 40123.
6. *Keesing's Record of World Events*, Vol. 40, No. 3, 1994, p. 39936.
7. *Keesing's Record of World Events*, Vol. 38, No. 1, 1992, p. 38709.
8. *Keesing's Record of World Events*, Vol. 38, No. 3, 1992, p. 38802.
9. Saad Eddin Ibrahim, "Crises, Elites, and Democratization in the Arab World," *Middle East Journal*, Vol. 47, No. 2, Spring 1993, p. 299.
10. Dankwart Rustow, "Democracy: A Global Revolution?" *Foreign Affairs*, Vol. 69, No. 4, 1990, p. 78.
11. Ibrahim, "Crises, Elites . . . ," p. 293.
12. *Middle East International*, No. 17, 1989, p. 3; *New York Times*, March 11, 1990, pp. 1 & 18.
13. "Egypt," *The Middle East and North Africa 1993*, 39th ed. (London: Europa Publications Ltd., 1992), p. 379.
14. Ibid, p. 381.
15. Personal interview with a Shura Council candidate who requested anonymity, New York City, January 1991.
16. Reasons for the boycott and the opposition's demands were presented in opposition newspapers such as *al-Sha`b* and *al-Wafd*.
17. John Lancaster, "Fundamentalists Jailed Before Egypt's Election: Candidates, Others Convicted of Political Acts," *The Washington Post*, November 24, 1995, p. 14.
18. "Egypt: Hundreds of Brotherhood Supporters Arrested," *al- Hayat*, November 28, 1995, p. 1.
19. Muhammad Ahmad Krar, *Intikhabat wa Barlamanat al-Sudan* (The Elections and Parliaments of Sudan) (Khartoum: Institute of Research and Social Studies, 1989), p. 138.
20. "Election Watch," *Journal of Democracy*, January 1993, p. 132.
21. John Esposito and James Pistcatori, "Democratization and Islam," *Middle East Journal*, Vol. 45, No. 3, Summer 1991, p. 431.
22. Rashid al-Ghannouchi, "Al-Dimoqratiyya wal Wad` al-Tunisi" (Democracy and the Tunisian Situation), *al-Insan*, No. 8, Aug. 1992, p. 64.
23. Personal interview with source in close contact with Yemeni Islamists.
24. *Al-Dustur* (Jordanian daily newspaper), December 5, 1993, p.11.
25. Michael Hudson, "After the Gulf War: Prospects for Democratization in the Arab World," *Middle East Journal*, Vol. 45, No. 3, Summer 1991, p. 417.
26. "Election Watch," *Journal of Democracy*, April 1992, p. 122.

4

The Islamist Challenge

In order to understand why democratization has stalled at the same time that the appeal of Islamists has increased, it is important to study the characteristics of the Islamist challenge. The Islamist movement is not the latest reaction against modernity of an underdeveloped people led by fanatics whose beliefs are incompatible with democracy. The Islamist movement is a complex and diffuse social and political movement with some radical branches, consciously developing a substantive critique of the existing power structure. It is the refusal of the ruling elites and their supporters at home and abroad to tolerate such a critique or to allow its advocates to enter the political process that has stalled democratization. This chapter will describe Islamists in the Arab world, the history of their emergence, and the agendas they bring, in order to make clear the relationship of Islamization to democratization.

Who Are the Islamists?

The "Islamic movement," broadly speaking, includes all individuals and groups seeking to change their societies by deriving their ideology from Islam. While these groups and individuals differ in methods, approaches, styles, and substantive issues, they agree on the positive worth of Islam and the relevance of its basic concepts and values to the contemporary world. They want to shift the frame of reference in the public realm to one in which Islam, in its various interpretations, is a major shaping force. In this section, I will not discuss those groups which confine themselves to missionary work, such as al-Tabligh (a group whose members go door to door proselytizing Islam and do not believe in direct political activism.) The Islamic groups under study are those which call for the establishment of an "Islamic state" as a religious duty as well as a practical necessity.

Contemporary Islamic groups in the Arab world owe much to the Muslim Brotherhood (al-Ikhwan al Muslimun), founded in Egypt in 1927 by

Hasan al-Banna. In fact, most are either continuations or branches of the Brotherhood (in Egypt, Syria, Jordan, the Gulf states), split from the original Brotherhood (al-Jihad in Egypt and Palestine), or influenced by its teachings and experiences (Algeria's Islamic Salvation Front). The Muslim Brotherhood (Ikhwan) distinguished itself from its predecessors with three features. First, the Brotherhood went beyond preaching to form an activist organization. Building one of the most broadly based movements in Egypt and the Arab world is one of Banna's achievements. By the beginning of the 1950s, according to an early study, the Brotherhood had 1,500 branches throughout Egypt, with over a million actively registered members.[1] As for the spread of the movement outside Egypt, branches had sprung in Syria, Palestine, Jordan, Iraq, and Sudan even before the assassination of its founder, Hasan al-Banna, in 1949, and the Brotherhood had established contact with individuals in Morocco.

The second distinguishing feature of the Ikhwan is its concept of Islam as comprehensive, encompassing all aspects of human endeavor. Islam, Banna writes, is "doctrine and worship, nationhood and citizenship, religion and state, spirituality and action, Qur'an and a sword."[2] One of the earliest studies of the Ikhwan noted in the 1950s that:

> it is the organization of a movement, the leading of a generation, the application of the principles of the Islamic system to government, politics, and social matters, putting them into operation as a binding constitution, besides defending them as true doctrine.[3]

The Ikhwan's belief in the comprehensive quality of Islam is manifest in their involvement in a variety of activities including spiritual worship, missionary work, economic and social services, intellectual debates, and so forth.

The third point of distinction is the Brotherhood's emphasis on political action. "Bear in mind that you have two fundamental goals," Banna instructed the membership: "One, that the Islamic fatherland be freed from all foreign domination, and two, that a free Islamic state may arise in this free fatherland, acting according to the precepts of Islam, applying its social regulations, proclaiming its sound principles, and broadcasting its sage mission to all mankind."[4] These three characteristics established the Brotherhood as a unique and groundbreaking organization in the Muslim world.

The Islamic Resurgence

The Muslim Brotherhood played a role in the nationalist struggle in the late 1940s and early 1950s. For instance, the Egyptian, Syrian, and Jordanian branches of the Brotherhood formed a voluntary militia which fought in the war of 1948 against the Zionist militia. The Egyptian Brotherhood carried on a guerrilla war in 1951 against Britain's continued occupation of part of Egypt.[5] Despite the common ground between the Ikhwan and Nasser's Arab nationalism, however, the Egyptian Brotherhood clashed with Nasser. At first the Ikhwan welcomed the coup which overthrew King Faruk and established a republican system, but they quickly discovered that Nasser had an agenda that diverged significantly from their own. After an assassination attempt on his life which he attributed to the Brothers, Nasser dissolved the Ikhwan organization, imprisoned thousands of members, and hanged some of its leaders in 1954 and 1965.

The 1950s and early 1960s belonged to Nasser. Despite Nasser's use of Islam to legitimize his policies, especially his foreign policy, he spoke the language of Arab nationalism and Arab socialism in a clearly secular tone. Nasser's early successes in nationalizing the Suez Canal Company, standing up to the British, French, and Israeli aggression in 1956, his leadership role in the creation of the nonaligned movement, his strong (at least rhetorical) commitment to Arab unity and the restoration of Palestine, and finally, his indefatigable charisma, all made him the most popular Arab leader during this period. All these accomplishments provided Nasser with the legitimacy to pursue his goals and allowed him brutally to suppress any opposition. The Muslim Brotherhood was one such opposition.

After the Ikhwan in Egypt had ceased to be a viable political player, it was able to survive and function (amid varying degrees of intolerance) in Syria, Jordan, Sudan, and Iraq. However, even in those countries, Islamists were competing with nationalist movements other than Nasserism. In Syria and Iraq, for example, Islamists competed against the Ba`th Party, which captured power in 1963 in both these states. After the failure of the first "unity" experiment between Syria and Egypt from 1958–1961, Ba`thist control of power in Syria and Iraq gave another boost to the concept of Arab unity. However, local interests proved stronger than the abstract goal of unity. Talk of unification of these three nationalist countries (Syria, Iraq, and Egypt) produced no material result.

In fact, there was a gradual decline in the performance of nationalist regimes on all fronts. Nasser's assertive involvement in the internal affairs of other Arab countries and his venture in Yemen's Civil War exacerbated intra-Arab rivalries. The rigid and underplanned attempts at socialism in land reform and nationalization of most industries were not effective in reducing inequalities among people in those countries which implemented them. Finally, the most emphatically professed goal of the nationalist regimes, resistance to Israel and restoration of Palestinian rights, received a devastating blow with the defeat of Egypt, Jordan, and Syria in what is known as the Six Day War of 1967. Despite efforts by the nationalist regimes to minimize the impact of the loss,[6] this defeat became a turning point in the history of the Arab people. Historian Albert Hourani observes that the 1967 defeat was widely regarded as being not only a military loss but a kind of moral judgement. "If the Arabs had been defeated so quickly, completely, and publicly, might it not be a sign there was something rotten in their societies and in the moral system which they expressed?"[7] Hourani points to a real gap which came to exist between the elite and the masses. The masses expressed their hopes and grievances in a different language—the language of Islam. "Behind this [the problem of communication] there lay another problem, that of identity: What was the moral bond between them, by virtue of which they could claim to be a society and a political community?"[8] The significance of 1967 lies not only in that it precipitated the disillusionment of the masses with "imported" ideologies such as socialism and secularism, but that it brought back to center stage the debate over Islam as a source of identity and ideology.[9]

Although 1967 can be considered a moment in the Arab world when skepticism about dominant ideologies dawned and doubts about those regimes which propagated them multiplied, it would take another decade for Islamic groups to gather enough critical mass to become a challenge to Arab states. There are several reasons for the delay. First among them is the coming into power of a new set of rulers at the end of the 1960s. The 1970s began with the death of Nasser and the peaceful transition to Sadat's Egypt. Changes of leadership also occurred in Libya, Sudan, and South Yemen in 1969. In all three cases, a younger generation of leaders claimed to infuse new hope into radical Arab nationalism. In South Yemen's case the new hope was provided by strident Marxism. Only one year earlier, the Ba`th, led by Saddam Hussein, had recaptured power in Iraq. In 1970, Hafez Asad toppled his rivals and led Syria into a more pragmatic and cautious political role.

Thus, between 1968 and 1970, new leadership across the Arab world brought changes in orientation and policies. It would take some time before people could identify the direction of those in power. In the short term, all these regimes pledged to stay the course of Arab nationalism. An attempt to form a unified quad out of Syria, Egypt, Libya and Sudan was presented as an indication of the new leaders' commitment to the idea of Arab unity. However, after Sudan withdrew, the only sign of the new "union" was a building in Cairo in which a few bureaucrats continued to receive salaries until the late 1970s.

Nonetheless, the success of both Egypt and Syria in the initial stages of the 1973 war boosted the legitimacy of these new regimes. A degree of solidarity among all Arab states was demonstrated in the willingness of the traditionalist regimes (e.g. Saudi Arabia) to use oil as a weapon against those Western countries which supported Israel. The decision of Arab oil-producing countries to use the oil embargo against Western nations quadrupled the price of oil. Therefore, the oil-producing countries witnessed an "oil boom" which put large amounts of cash in the hands of the leaders of these nations. While most of this surplus would be recycled as investments in the West, or wasted on buying guns and luxury consumer goods from the West, some of this wealth was invested back in the oil-producing countries, and some was given to the countries on the Israeli front. This produced a period of high economic growth in most Arab countries. For example, the annual growth rate for most Arab countries in the 1970s was from 5 percent (Egypt) to over 10 percent (Saudi Arabia and the United Arab Emirates). This growth was not distributed equally, nor did it happen in a balanced way in all sectors of the economy. In Syria, for example, most of the revenues went to the defense budget and to investments that strengthened the coercive mechanisms of the regime. Overall, however, the limited Arab success in the war of 1973 and the oil boom provided most Arab regimes with some leverage that would appease their populations and delay popular dissatisfaction with the established powers.

As early as the 1980s, most Arab countries, including some of the oil-producing states, entered a period of economic crisis. There was a sharp decline in oil prices beginning in 1981–1982. Increased migration into urban centers put pressure on government services that were already unable to cope with the needs of the population. The spread of education, which had been facilitated by the boom years, produced a generation with more credentials than jobs, more expectations than opportunities. Governments did not know how to provide for the frustrated young—and youth made up over 60 percent of the population in most Arab countries. It is in this context of economic hardship, social alienation, political authoritarianism and the erosion of the legitimacy of Arab regimes that Islamic groups have made a strong comeback.

It is no accident, then, that many scholars explain the rise of Islamic "fundamentalism" in terms of the crisis theory. That is, writers who range from conservative to neo-Marxist describe "fundamentalism" in the Arab world as a reactionary response to the deteriorating socioeconomic and political conditions. A representative view is that of Halim Barakat:

> The vacuum created by the failure of Arab nationalism and Arab socialism seems to have encouraged certain segments of the middle class and the lower middle classes to resort to an old political weapon. Other conditions have contributed to the revival of Arab religious fundamentalism as a polit-

> ical movement: enduring economic crises, social anomie, distorted modernization, deliberate manipulation and even sponsorship of religious movements by some governments, and tyranny of the state over civil society.[10]

It is not clear how disenfranchised classes, in accepting Islamist ideas, can be said to resort to an "old political weapon" when they do not control the means of manipulation or communication; they do not have "weapons." Nor is it clear how Islamists can be considered the sponsorees of some governments when they are subject to repressive measures in nearly every Arab country.

In any case, context is not cause, and while it is important to understand the environment in which Islamic movements have gained widespread acceptance among Arab populations, the "crisis" argument cannot adequately explain the challenge posed by these movements. Such explanations ignore the fact that Islamic movements existed long before the current crisis, and had a significant following long before they hit the front pages of the Western media or the agenda-books of post–Cold War US policymakers. Views such as Barakat's explain Islamists today as if they were without a history, as if they sprang overnight from the desperation of a gullible underclass. Islamists in several countries have a decades-long record of providing social services to the public. Egypt's Muslim Brotherhood had over one million members in the late 1940s. One million members is not a bad showing, long before the crisis of 1967 or the post 1970s economic bust.

What happened in the intervening decades is that Islamists became less visible within Arab countries, in large part because they were suppressed by authoritarian regimes. On the world stage, much of their invisibility was due to the preoccupation of the Cold War powers with issues of bipolar conflict. During this time, Islamic movements nevertheless continued to function and to grow, working less on political activities and more on social services and the production of ideas. When an Islamist organization was repressed in one Arab country, it would move its activities to another country, taking advantage of the hidden blessings of Arab disunity.

The "crisis theory" neglects the history of Islamic movements on the one hand, and is unwilling to see a future for them on the other. This theory assumes that Islamic resurgence is a temporary phenomenon arising in response to material needs which have been rationalized in religious-superstitious terms. If economic problems are solved, the implication is, Islamists will fade away. This paradigm assumes that material needs are basic and ideological needs superficial or secondary, whereas one may just as well advance that:

> there are meta-needs that may not be as pressing but are probably more enduring than those basic needs. It is these meta-needs that can motivate an

> individual to sacrifice his very life in the service of what is perceived as Ultimate Reality, call it God, Allah, or by any other name; and it is this capacity for self-sacrifice that forms the basis of intergenerational transfer of values which is the essence of the making of a civilization.[11]

Proponents of the "crisis theory" are often reluctant to admit that their grounds for excluding Islamists in their vision of the future are as arbitrary as their assumptions about the universality of their hierarchy of needs.

Moreover, the "crisis theory" is mainly concerned with explaining the rise of radical, especially violent, Islamists. It has little to offer in explaining the widespread existence of moderate and middle-class Islamists, whose existence is often not even acknowledged in the "crisis theory" of the Islamist movement.

As an explanation for the origin and development of the Islamist movement in all its diverse forms, the "crisis theory" advanced in the main by leftist scholars is not useful. On the other hand, socioeconomic crisis is important in constituting one context to which Islamists, who precede "crisis," respond in forming their agendas. Also, socioeconomic crisis may be an explanatory factor when one asks why the methods of different types of Islamists varies, e.g. why peasant-based groups (*gama`at*) in southern rural Egypt tend toward violent methods while the Islah parties in the Gulf states produce children's song-tapes and focuses on education.

Another major deficiency in understanding the Islamic resurgence is the lack of knowledge, or the presence of biased knowledge, about Islam and its social expressions in history. Scholars from a spectrum of political persuasions operating within a Western intellectual tradition tend to treat religious faith as universally discredited, because of that tradition's deep conflicts with religion. In their eyes, anyone whose political ideology derives from religious beliefs is equated with the kind of fundamentalism popularly seen in the West as literalist, escapist and reactionary. Islam, however, has remained integrated in the historical process in the Muslim world; it has remained a source of energy in social and intellectual life and has not been segregated from public life. Current expressions of political Islam are manifestations of what John Esposito describes as "faith-in-history," "the product of a dynamic changing process in which the word of revelation is mediated through human discourse in response to specific sociohistorical contexts."[12] For Islamists, the resurgence of the late 1970s is a continuation of the process of responding to new sets of social, economic, and political conditions, similar to previous resurgences in which Islam was the prime ideological resource; they see this as a fulfillment of the Prophet's saying that "every hundred years God sends to this *umma* someone who rejuvenates its way of life." Whether it is mined for the resources needed to resist Crusaders in the twelfth century or to mobilize the masses against European imperialism in the nineteenth, Islam has been the ideological bedrock of the Arab world and there is no reason to expect it not to continue to be so. Indeed, the question "Why Islamic awakening?" is not a neutral one but is based on certain normative assumptions. One could equally assume that it is the normal status for Muslims to be in a state of *sahwa* (awakening), in a constant creative interpretation of Islam's role in the temporal world. The question then becomes, "What factors had operated to alienate Muslims in the Arab world from Islam before this moment?" Then the investigation of Islamic resurgence "changes from one about the factors external and internal which led to a renewed widespread commitment to Islam, into an inquiry into the pressures to which Muslims were subjected in order to abandon their faith."[13]

To summarize the argument thus far, attempts at modernization and nation-building in the decades following Arab independence from colonial rule had been carried out under the banner of Arab nationalism, frequently in some combination with Arab socialism, in terms that were both secularized and Westernized. It was a period in which the dominant elites in most of the Arab world were speaking a different language, metaphorically and in some countries literally, than the masses, who were largely excluded from the political process. The deliberate and forcible exclusion of Islam as a source of ideology and of Islamists as a social base from most of those experiments, and the failure of the nationalist regimes to live up to their promises, failure culminating in the total defeat of 1967, provoked the Arab people to reassess the bases of their identity and the role of Islam in it. While there were multiple answers, the idea that the Arab malaise was related to the displacement of Islam as a primary source of ideology steadily gained acceptance throughout the 1970s. With it came the notion that only Islam could provide the cultural resources needed to formulate an alternative to Western hegemony and "imported ideologies."[14]

By the late 1970s, signs of Islamic resurgence were apparent throughout the Arab world. Anyone travelling anywhere from Mauritania to Iraq could not but observe increased religious observance among the populations. Indications included growing prayer attendance at mosques, proliferation of religious books and tapes, and the rising popularity of new Islamic forms of dress among women.

The success of the Islamic Revolution in Iran gave a psychological boost to most Islamically oriented groups and individuals. The significance of the Iranian revolution was not in its attempts to export the revolution to Arab countries, but in its demonstrative effect. It showed how an oppressive authoritarian regime such as that of the Shah could be defeated despite the odds, and even despite the support of the world's strongest power, the United States. The Iranians pioneered the "Islamization of revolution," revealing the power of Islam as a mobilizing factor. Although no Arab state has experienced a comparable revolution, there have been attempts, such as the clashes following Sadat's assassination in 1981 and the efforts of the Syrian Ikhwan to topple the Asad regime from 1979 to 1982.

It was only after this period that governments began in earnest to search Islam for language and symbols that would buttress their legitimacy and appropriate for them some of the popularity of Islamists. Three cases will give a representative idea of this phenomenon. Asad introduced an article into the Constitution of Syria indicating that the religion of the President of Syria should be Islam. This after Asad had tried to omit any reference to Islam in his proposed draft of the Constitution in 1973. At that time, following a wave of protests and demonstrations, especially among the *ulama*, he reluctantly reinstated the clause and quickly instructed the Grand Mufti to issue a *fatwa* declaring the Alawite religion a branch of Shi`ism. This move would make the Alawites mainstream Muslims. (The secretive Alawite religion, a splinter off Shi`i Islam, had been and still is widely regarded as outside of mainstream Islam.)[15] A second example of governmental manipulation of Islam is Sadat's 1980 amendment of the Egyptian Constitution making *shari`a* (Islamic law) the main source of legislation. Even before that, Sadat had named himself *al-ra'is al-mu'min* (the Believer President). A third example: Sudan's Ja`far al-Numayri turned to Islam to salvage his deteriorating popularity in the late 1970s. Then between 1983 and 1984 he carried out a noisy campaign of Islamization through the literal implementation of Islamic law, especially the penal code. His policies, while they were met with popular acceptance among Muslims in the North, generated a great deal of controversy and criticism. Given the subsequent overthrow of Numayri by pro-Islamist forces, this shows that the scheme of manipulating Islam to improve a leader's legitimacy could backfire by exposing his hypocrisy. As Esposito points out: "Those who wield it [Islamic rhetoric] run the risk of being judged by that Islamic yardstick, challenged or toppled."[16]

Increased religious observance among the masses and governmental co-optation of Islamic symbols and language are only minor manifestations of the Islamic resurgence. The real dynamic force behind the resurgence has been Islamist groups and organizations. From their marginal status in the political arena in the 1950s and 1960s, Islamist groups rose as political players by the late 1970s. It is probably accurate to say that by the early 1980s Islamists had become the popular trend. There is virtually no Arab country without a strong Islamic movement, as Table 4.1 shows.

TABLE 4.1 Major Islamic Groups in Some Arab Countries

Country	*Islamic Groups*
Algeria	Islamic Salvation Front (FIS); Islamic Society Movement; Renaissance (Al-Nahda)
Bahrain	Social Reform Organization (Al-Islah); various shi`i groups
Egypt	Muslim Brotherhood (Ikhwan); Islamic Jihad; The Islamic Group (Al-Gama`a al-Islamiyya); the Labor Party (Al-`Amal); small groups
Iraq	Islamic Call (Al-Da`wah); Muslim Brotherhood
Jordan	Islamic Action Front; Muslim Brotherhood; Liberation Party (Al-Tahrir)
Kuwait	Islamic Constitutional Movement; small Salafi & Shi`i groups
Lebanon	Party of God (Hizbullah); Islamic Group (Al-Jama`a al-Islamiyya)
Libya	Muslim Brotherhood
Morocco	Justice and Charity Association; Muslim Youth Movement
Palestine	Islamic Resistance Movement (Hamas); Islamic Jihad
Saudi Arabia	Salafi groups; Muslim Brotherhood
Sudan	National Islamic Front
Syria	Muslim Brotherhood; small groups
Tunisia	Renaissance Party (Al-Nahda)
U.A.E.	Social Reform and Guidance (Al-Islah)
Yemen	Yemeni Alliance for Reform (Al-Islah)

Sources: Data compiled from various issues of *Al-Mujtama`*; *Al-Islah*; *Al-Sha`b*; *Al-Da`wa*, 1990–1995.

Islamist Agendas[17]

It is important to shed some light on the Islamist groups, their agendas, the socioeconomic background of their members, and their positions on democracy, in order to determine what kind of a challenge they constitute to the current order. The starting point for Islamist groups is that the Arab world is in a state of decline; the idea of Arab nationalism in its secular forms not only failed to provide a way out, but aggravated the problems; and "Islam" is the only viable and authentic solution to these problems. All Islamic groups seek to transform Arab societies and polities into more "Islamic" ones, although there is a debate over what that entails. This process of Islamization does not mean that Islamic movements reject modern ideas out-of-hand. Robin Wright, for example, sees a resemblance between Islamists and Catholic liberation movements which harmonize religious beliefs with modern thought to impart a vision of betterment for people in the temporal world as well as the moral realm. Islamists, she says, carry out "forward-looking, interpretive and often even innovative attempts to reconstruct the social order."[18]

It has often been noted that Islamists are quite flexible about adopting Western technologies and scientific achievements, but they think Western knowledge, values, and structures can be adopted only after being "Islamized," or sifted to determine which elements are compatible with Islam and which are not. This position is different from that of earlier Muslim reformers such as Muhammad Abduh. As Islamists view it, Abduh strove to make Islam compatible with modernity while Islamists strive to make modernity compatible with Islam.

A second point about Islamists is that they share many of the concerns of Arab nationalist movements, despite their criticism of nationalist ideologies. Islamists do not disagree with Arab nationalists on what constitutes the main issues of concern to Arab peoples. Sheikh Yusuf al-Qaradawi, an advocate of "the Islamic solution," identifies these main issues of concern to Islamists: underdevelopment and backwardness; social injustice; political despotism; dependency and Westernization; deterioration of Arab strength vis-à-vis Israel; the fragmentation of the Arab world; and moral degeneracy in Arab society.[19] This list does not diverge all that much from the concerns of many Arab nationalists.

Islamist groups within and across countries differ in the methods they use to pursue their professed goals and in the sophistication with which they treat the task of socioeconomic and political change. While there are some Islamist groups which espouse the use of violence for political ends (such as Egypt's al-Gama`a al-Islamiyya and armed Islamist militias in Algeria), the majority of Islamist organizations pursue their goals peacefully, using a variety of reformist methods.

For the extremist groups, the struggle to overthrow corrupt and illegitimate governments is a religious duty, a part of the larger concept of *jihad*. It is a struggle between right and wrong, good and evil, faith and unbelief. In such a conflict, they believe violent means are a legitimate recourse for the oppressed and the powerless. According to a scholar of Egyptian radical groups, they employ violence to prove their existence on the political map, to exact revenge against the state's security apparatus for killing and suppressing their members, and to demonstrate the political instability of the regime and consequently weaken it.[20]

There are three critical points to be made about the radical groups. One, most of these groups have resorted to violence as a result of intense suppression and coercion by the most authoritarian regimes in the Arab world. For example, in Asad's Syria, one of the world's most severe authoritarian systems, the Alawite-dominated regime has long prevented any meaningful participation by the Sunni majority. Syria's Muslim Brotherhood was radicalized by Asad's brutality. Some of Egypt's radical Islamic groups splintered from the Muslim Brotherhood during the last years of Nasser's rule, a time when the state unleashed extreme terror against the Brotherhood and many of its leaders were imprisoned, tortured, and executed. These groups were further alienated by the continuation of authoritarian rule under Sadat and Mubarak. In the Algerian case, the groups affiliated with FIS resorted to violence only after the elections that the Islamists won by a landslide were rescinded. In their view, they are themselves the duly elected rulers and the military junta is the violent usurper of legitimate state power and thus they have the same authority to use violence against this regime as a state would have to use its police or army to fight armed insurgents.

Second, radical Islamist groups tend not to have a clear program of what they want to achieve. Among the small Islamic groups in Egypt, the dominant discourse is how to fight oppression inflicted by the unjust Arab rulers. This is an interesting development since Sunni tradition is usually characterized as lacking revolutionary spirit compared to Shi`ism; Sunni scholarly tradition justifies submission to the existing order as long as rulers use Islamic symbols. This had not worked for Sadat; although he invoked Islam to gain acceptance and legitimacy, he was assassinated by al-Jihad, a group which believes in toppling rulers who do not implement *Shari`a* as an utmost priority. The chief theorist of Jihad, Muhammad Abdussalam Faraj, who was executed after the assassination, wrote a tract representative of the discourse of radical Islamists, entitled *Al-Farida al-Gha'iba* (The Forgotten Obligation). The forgotten obligation among Muslims today, he says, is *jihad* or fighting against oppression:

> We must concentrate on our Islamic mission. This mission is, first of all, to establish the Law of God (*shari`a*) in our land and to raise up the Word of God as the highest. No doubt the first task of *jihad* is to uproot these infidel leaders and replacing them with the comprehensive Islamic system. This will be our starting point.[21]

Third, there seem to be similarities in the socioeconomic background of members of radical Islamist groups, and these groups tend to be small. While the size of radical groups varies from one country to another, most are small; for example, Jihad had no more than a few hundred members in 1981.[22] However, the number of such groups has proliferated in Egypt due to the failure of the Mubarak regime to address the grievances of the majority of Egyptians. In the case of Algeria, on the other hand, the number of armed groups is estimated in the tens of thousands. Most of the members of radical groups are young, educated in modern institutions, and lower to middle class. If we take the 101 members of Jihad who were brought to courts after the assassination of Sadat, we find that about 75 percent were between 20–29 years of age. A fourth were professionals, 45 percent students, 15 percent workers, 5 percent owners of bookstores, 4 percent army recruits and police officers, 2 percent farmers and 3.9 percent unemployed.[23] This is what leads Saad Eddin Ibrahim, who has done much research on radical Islamists, to remark that "[it] is sometimes assumed in social science that recruits of 'radical movements' must be somehow alienated, marginal, or otherwise abnormal. Most of those we investigated would be considered model young Egyptians."[24]

The majority of Islamist groups in the Arab world have proposed to transform the dismal conditions in their societies by working from below, beginning at the grass roots level, through peaceful means. Most follow the reformist methods of Banna which emphasize gradual change beginning with the individual. In other words, they believe that individual Muslims must reform themselves; that reformed Muslims can then work for the reform of whole families and raise the Islamic consciousness of their society; and that only when society is ready to accept Islam freely can the state be reformed along Islamic principles. Islamists of the 1990s who belong to a third generation of active Islamist reform see themselves as *tayyar al-wasat* (the middle or moderate wave). They are modernist rather than traditionalist in experience and outlook. A significant number of these Islamists have Western educations; many hold degrees in the prestigious professions of medicine and the hard sciences and dominate in the professional unions. The moderate Islamists include the Muslim Brotherhood in Egypt, the Islamic Action Front in Jordan, Al-Nahda (Renaissance) of Tunisia, early FIS (before its repression by the military) and the Islamic Society Movement in Algeria, the Yemeni Alliance for Reform (Islah), and other Islamists in the Gulf states.

What do these movements have in common with the radical Islamist groups and where do they differ? They agree on the general goal of trying to make Islamic values the main source of identity and the main criteria for legislation. They differ on the pace and method of implementation, but this divergence also reveals substantive differences. Radical Islamists proclaim their desire to implement "Islam" as soon as they gain power. Moderates not only see the Islamization of society as a gradual process, but one that takes into serious consideration local contexts. Their view of what society would look like at the end of the process is more pluralistic than the radical Islamist view. The other major difference is about the use of force to bring about the Islamic order. On this issue, each side has condemned the other's tactics. For the radicals, participation in the existing system and attempting to change it from within is an exercise in futility because the ruling elite will never allow such change to be completed. For the moderates, using violence is counterproductive and only hinders the Islamization process by confirming the stereotypes of Islamists as fanatic and giving justification to the regime for their continued repression. This is why the moderate groups use the following methods: Preaching Islam on the individual level (*da`wa*); building economic institutions (e.g. Islamic banks and credit unions) as both a source of income and an alternative to state institutions; providing educational and social services, such as free health care, to the populace, particularly to the lowest strata; pressuring governments to implement *shari`a;* working toward greater influence in various organs of civil society, such as professional and student unions; and entering the political process by participating in elections whenever they are allowed.

Islamist Positions Toward Democracy

One area of disagreement between radical and moderate Islamists is their positions on democracy, both in theory and in what limited democratic practices have been available to them. Radical groups and some traditionalist scholars tend to reject democracy as an "imported," meaning inherently Western and somehow unIslamic, theory of government. Most Islamists, on the other hand, conceive of themselves as reformers of society by gradual means: education, social change, preaching, and working within the system. Once they get past the Western terminology and the Western models to the basic concepts, values, and procedures of democracy, they find it entirely compatible with Islam, descriptive of beliefs they already hold, and indeed capable of best expressing Islamic values in political life.

The radicals' argument contains three grounds for rejecting democracy. The first is the supposed differences between Islamic political principles and democracy. In Islam, according to proponents of this view, sovereignty belongs to God and not to the people. Sayyid Qutb and his brother Muhammad insist on this distinction between two types of governments: those based on Islam and those based on *jahiliyya* (ignorance, or pre-Islamic degeneracy). Under Islamic rule the right of people to legislate is limited by *Shari`a.* The representatives of the people cannot pass a law which contradicts a law prescribed by God. According to this school, allowing any humans or group of humans unlimited power to legislate is a form of tyranny and a component of *jahiliyya.* The only way to achieve real freedom is under an "Islamic" rule whereby no human is entitled to become the sovereign—to hold absolute power of legislation.[25] Islam has its own unique political system, these Islamists assert, which is better than any other one, including "democracy." Muhammad Qutb, while acknowledging what he calls positive elements in democratic systems (such as the rights and guarantees of the people against the abuse of power by rulers), insists that "Islam" is the ideal system and not "democracy." Those positive elements of democracy that are compatible with the

Islamic system, he says, should not make us lose track of the fact that it is not a divinely ordained system, while Islam is. One cannot abandon a divinely ordained system for an imperfect man-made one; that would signal the defeat of our system of thought, he cautions, and the triumph of the Western paradigm. To those who say "let us take what is best in democracy," Muhammad Qutb would say, then it will not be democracy, but Islam.[26]

In recent years, Islamists in general have emphasized the idea that Islam is their frame of reference (*al-marji`iyya al-Islamiyya*). Even those who are willing to adopt Western ideas and systems find it necessary to justify them in Islamic terms. This reflects an increase in Islamists' confidence that they represent an alternative paradigm, complete with its own set of referents, rather than an enterprise that needs to frame itself within a set of referents from Western intellectual traditions.

The second ground radical groups cite for rejecting democracy is its connection to things Western, which makes it suspect. Conventional wisdom about democracy among Islamists has it, for example, that Western claims about the people's rule are disingenuous, that it is economically powerful groups who rule, and that elections are rituals that do not present genuine choices between substantively different policies. Another common idea is that democracy is responsible for the moral decay and sexual promiscuity which prevail in the West today. The author of a small book entitled *Hukm al-Islam fil Dimoqratiyya* (Islam's Judgement on Democracy) asserts that the equivalent term in Arabic for democracy is *ibahiyya* (laxity, permissiveness), which means an erasure of all boundaries and the freedom to do the things God forbids, from drinking, adultery, and homosexuality, to apostasy.[27]

More persuasively, some Islamists point out that "democracy," from where Arabs sit, has direct historical associations with Western imperialism, with the colonization of Arab lands and its aftermath. Proponents of this view doubt the sincerity of Western efforts to propagate democracy and see these efforts as invested in Western political interests. Democracy did not stop European countries from colonizing and brutalizing the Arab world in the past, despite Western claims that it is an ideology of individual rights, egalitarianism, self-determination, and enlightened morality. Nor did democracy prevent the United States from destroying Baghdad in a military intervention resented by most Arab populations. The Gulf war significantly increased cynicism among Islamists about the value of democracy.[28] There is something suspect about Western nations' insistence on "democracy" from the point of view of many formerly colonized peoples, who note the relief with which Algeria's military coup was welcomed in the democratic West. Western powers are trying to interest Arabs in "democratic values," some Islamists reason, so as to produce Arab systems that are pliantly pro-Western and will support neoimperialist Western hegemony in the region.

The third reason why some Islamists reject "democracy" is that their perception of democracy loses its luster when people observe how "democracy" is implemented in various Arab countries. When Islamists, representing some of the most politicized groups in a country, are excluded from the political process, "democracy" starts to look like just another corrupt ideology. Thus some of the radical groups in Egypt extend their cynicism about the democratic process in their country to the idea of "democracy" in general. Several documents published by the radical Islamist groups posit democracy as the opposite of Islam.[29] Similarly, the theorist of the Jihad group writes, "Power is the only path for the return of Islam. We reject the idea that one can reform the system by accepting appointments and offices in government. We reject also the idea that one must establish a wide popular base through *da`wa* (propagating Islam) as the path to establishing the Islamic state."[30]

Groups which subscribe to this position on democracy are a minority within Islamist circles in the Arab world today. These groups are Egypt's al-Gama`a al-Islamiyya and Jihad, and Jordan's small, strident Liberation (Tahrir) Party. There are some persons in moderate Islamist groups who ascribe, as individuals, to the radical hard line against "democracy," notably some members of Algeria's FIS Fahmi Huwaidi, an independent Islamist writer, agrees that the discourse of such individuals is an anomaly and is circumscribed among the wider circle of Islamists. This anomalous view and its proponents receive most of the attention of regional and world media, to the degree that the antidemocracy view has come to be seen as the Islamist norm while the views of the majority of Islamists appear exceptional.[31]

Most of the mainstream Islamist organizations were formed in the first place on the premise that their task is to transform society by working within existing institutions. When they have been afforded the opportunity to participate in democratic processes, they have been willing to do so. Islamist commitment to the democratic process has developed out of three factors. First, Islamists all across the Arab world have suffered a great deal at the hands of the *Mukhabarat* (secret police). They know first hand the costs of authoritarianism. Many of their leaders and cadres were assassinated, imprisoned, tortured, executed, or sentenced to exile. Among the most prominent in Egypt, for example: Hasan al-Banna, founder of the Muslim Brotherhood, was assassinated by King Faruk's agents; Sayyid Qutb and a band of other Ikhwan leaders were executed under Nasser; Zainab al-Ghazali and other activists were subjected to torture in Nasser's jails. Most surviving leaders of that generation of Egypt's Ikhwan served long prison terms. Leaders as well as ordinary members of Islamist organizations in Syria, Sudan, Tunisia, Algeria, Morocco, and other states have suffered prison terms and continue to do so; many others have been forced into exile, their property confiscated, their relatives who remain in their home country harassed. Even those who are not exiled live under surveillance and the constant threat of arbitrary state violence. This has made resistance to authoritarianism a strong component of the Islamist subculture. Islamists have developed a language, even a mythology, one might say, with its heroes and conflicts, of such resistance. Those who suffered prison terms became especially aware of the dangers of human rights abuses and the need for a system that will prevent such abuses; despotism is the greatest obstacle, in their view, to progress. They see despotism (*al- istibdad*) as "the giant obstacle in the path of . . . the Islamic movement—which has been the greatest victim of despotism," as Rashid al-Ghannouchi, ideologue of Tunisia's Islamic movement writes, pointing out Islamists' growing awareness of the evils of authoritarianism. This awareness was influenced, he says, by "the global wave of demands for democratization and the toppling of dictatorships" in recent years. The predisposition to accept concepts which happen to be components of democracy as understood in the West today, such as citizenship, the full participation of women in politics, and pluralism, is gaining momentum among Islamists. This is indicated by both their writings and their praxis in more than one country.[32]

The second reason why Islamists are advocating democracy is that they see it as a way to attain political power. Since it is supposed to lead to peaceful transfer of power in government, democracy, for any oppositional movement with a wide popular base, is the best means to the goal. Islamists are no exception; they "have not failed to recognize that pluralism and interdependence are the catchwords of the 1990s."[33] More importantly, Islamists realize that they have popular support and are running against governments that do not. It is not difficult to foresee the outcome of free and fair elections in such a setting. Although supporters and critics of Islamists alike have the right to demand guarantees of fairness in the electoral process, they have no democratic grounds on which to exclude Islamists from the process. There are those who argue for excluding Islamists from elections on the grounds that if Islamists come to power, they would destroy any further democracy. Questioning the commitment to democracy of oppositional groups is an evasion tactic (one which was also, by the way, used in Western countries to try to exclude leftist parties from elections). This exclusion is an obvious attempt to limit the range of ideological choices of the voters and thus begs the question of identity, which is in large part what draws Islamists into the process in the first place. The criticism often levelled by regime representatives as well as leftists, that Islamists have no business bringing religion into politics, begs this same question. The claim that Islamists should be excluded because they lack sophistication in formulating political platforms is also moot at this point. The fact of the matter is that Islamists, whatever their interpretation of religion's role in politics, constitute a political movement organized into political parties prepared to contest in elections in order to gain power and implement their programs. It is the task of other political parties to make sure that if this were to happen, Islamists would not suppress their opponents "in the name of Allah" or abolish the people's right periodically to choose their leaders in free and fair elections. Strengthening democratic institutions goes a great way toward ensuring this. Excluding Islamists now does not set good precedents for those who expect strong commitment to these institutions in the future. So far Islamists have been subjected to higher moral standards than the other players in the arena, as if they were the only authoritarians among an assembly of tried and true democrats.

Thirdly, mainstream Islamists increasingly accept the democratic process and the idea of democracy in general because they see it as more compatible with Islamic principles than any other form of government around. Those among Islamists who speak of congruity between Islamic principles and democracy[34] emphasize the idea that Islam does not prescribe any fixed organizational structure; such a task belongs to the community or *umma*. This community, which includes people of other religions, must form its own political systems. A multiple number of forms is possible, as long as they are based on the following principles:

1. The *raison d'être* of any Islamic state is to establish justice and to work for the prosperity of the community both in this life and the hereafter.
2. The authority of the rulers in any Islamic state is limited by the law (*shari`a*). No individual or institution can legislate anything that clearly contradicts the *shari`a*. Complications arise in those matters about which there is no clear ruling. Then it is the duty of all people of religious knowledge—without restriction—to conduct *ijtihad* (independent reasoning). When the community of scholars is able to reach a consensus, or *ijma`*, that consensus becomes binding on the rest of the community.

The limitation of legislative authority to the boundaries of *shari`a* is one point on which Islamist political principles seem to conflict with the idea of democracy as understood in the Western intellectual traditions. However, every society is limited by the boundaries of its collective historical experience; even the framers of the US Constitution conceived of the document they drafted as existing within the context of a "higher law." The boundaries of one's own cultural context seem invisible because they are tacit, diffuse, and accepted as the norm; they may be challenged, stretched, and reinterpreted, but boundaries nonetheless exist around every democratic system. The boundaries suggested by Islamists—specifically, *shari`a*—appear alien, heavy, and restrictive, not only to Western observers but even to some members of the Muslim societies in which they are proposed, precisely because their installment is the focus of the debate at hand. Islamists see a distinction between democracy as a set of procedural principles and democracy as an expression of Western values and a specifically Western heritage. It is the first package in which Islamists are interested and not the second.

3. The leader or leaders of the state should be chosen with the approval of the community. Members of the community express their acceptance of the choice by giving a pledge (*bay`a*). Contemporary Sunni Islamists disapprove of hereditary monarchy (despite that concept's longevity in the region) as it neglects the element of choice. They disagree also with contemporary Shi`i Islamists who maintain that the ruler must also be a descendent of the Prophet Muhammad and a religious scholar (*faqih*). There is general agreement among mainstream Islamists that elections constitute the best way for peoples to choose their leaders today.

4. Leaders should conduct politics according to the principle of consultation (*shura*); that is, leaders are obliged to consult the people or their representatives throughout the decision-making process.

5. Political participation is a religious duty for the individual believer, especially at two moments: choosing the most qualified person to lead the community, and voicing one's opinion in good conscience, often equated with the idea of bearing witness, during critical decisions that affect the community.

6. Islamists have begun turning their attention to the question of pluralism in recent years;[35] the general consensus has been acceptance of the principle of political pluralism (*ta`adudiyya*) as a natural tendency among people. Mainstream Islamists usually point out that the existence of at least four schools of jurisprudence in Sunni Islam is a strong argument for the tolerance of differences. Islamists disagree, however, on whether political parties constitute the best mechanism for channelling differences of opinion in the political domain.

7. There is agreement among most Islamists that the principle of separation among the branches of the political system is a sound development in government. While there is disagreement over whether a presidential or parliamentary system is better, or whether Islamists should develop an alternative system that would guarantee representative government in some other way, the necessity for a strong independent judiciary is basic to Islamist thought.

8. Contemporary Islamists conceptualize human rights and individual freedoms in Islamic terms by maintaining that these rights and freedoms are manifestations of God's will to dignify human beings regardless of

race, religion, or ethnicity. How these rights are defined is another issue. Islamist ideology may espouse many democratic values but it does so within limits that preserve a privileged position for religion. While the right to an honorable existence includes freedom from government interference, repression, and torture, "mainstream attitudes remain highly restrictive with regard to the freedom of political, religious, and artistic expression, if that involves the right to freely express one's religious feelings, doubts included, and even to give up Islam altogether."[36]

This is a distilling of key concepts from the volumes that have been written about Islamists and democracy. What follows is a survey of representative Islamist discourse on democracy.

Sheikh Muhammad al-Ghazali of Egypt's Islamist movement has been one of the most outspoken advocates of democracy.[37] Ghazali argues against those who see a contradiction between Islam and democracy. To him democracy is not a religion but a way to organize the relationship between the rulers and the governed, and a guarantee against the abuse of power. Making rulers accountable to those they govern and preventing arbitrary rule are common goals of democratic and Islamic principles. The fact that democracy relates to the process of government, rather than its substance, makes it reconcilable with *shari`a*, which is substantive.

Another proponent of democracy, human rights, and freedom in the Islamic resurgence is Rashid al-Ghannouchi, head of Tunisia's Islamist movement. In his latest book, *al-Huriyat al-`Amma fil Dawla al-Islamiyya* (Public Liberties in the Islamic State),[38] Ghannouchi reiterates his conviction that the struggle for freedom and the destruction of oppressive structures is a struggle for Islam. Democratic mechanisms such as free elections, peaceful transfer of power, decision-making through majority rule, and protection for the rights of minorities, are universally applicable, according to Ghannouchi. Nothing in these contradicts Islamic values. Furthermore, "if the democratic apparatus operated within a framework in which Christianity was dominant and produced Christian democracy, and within the framework of socialist philosophy produced socialist democracy, and within the framework of Jewish values produced Jewish democracy, is it then impossible for democracy to function in a framework of Islamic principles to produce Islamic democracy?" Such a development, Ghannouchi believes, would benefit not only the Muslim nation but the whole Arab world and "all humanity."[39] He goes on to make two points. First, any Islamic state should provide safety valves to guard civil and political liberties and prevent any form of despotism. Those who do not accept the notion that an Islamic order could be democratic are directly challenged by this argument. Ghannouchi adopts a bold interpretation of various Islamic texts with political content, and offers a progressive agenda in areas in which Islamists are frequently criticized. For instance, he advocates the political empowerment of women, recommending affirmative action to increase their representation in legislative bodies.[40] Second, while Ghannouchi would like to see Islamists reach the goal of establishing an Islamic order, he prefers to work for the creation of a pluralistic democratic system, especially where Muslims are not a majority or do not accept Islam as their frame of reference. In these conditions, "it is enough to create a political pact between Islamists and others in which all pledge loyalty to the state, renounce imposing their order through violence, and accept the peaceful transfer of government through the ballot box."[41] In such a system, it is enough to arrive at a consensus about public liberties and human rights. The democratic state, or, in Ibn Khaldun's vocabulary, rational government (*hukumat al-`aql*), is the closest form to the government of *shari`a*, Ghannouchi maintains. Would Ghannouchi and his party be willing to give up power peacefully if they lose an election? "Definitely," Ghannouchi answers. "I will withdraw to an oppositional position, prepare myself, and run again. If I am rejected, I will try again."[42]

One of the most widely respected scholars among mainstream Islamists, Sheikh Yusuf al-Qaradawi, issued a religious ruling (*fatwa*) in response to those who claim that democracy is a form of unbelief (*kufr*). The text of the *fatwa*, running over sixteen pages, can be summarized as follows:[43] First, those who claim democracy is *kufr* understand neither Islam nor democracy. The essence of democracy, according to Qaradawi, is for people to choose their leaders and system without compulsion, to have the right to question their leaders if they make mistakes, and to depose them if they deviate from the agreed-upon pact. Second, the main virtue of democracy lies, as a result of long struggles with oppressors and despots, in its procedures and mechanisms for protecting the populace from tyrants. Third, Islam has some abstract principles, such as *shura*, which need to be institutionalized, and requires believers to search for a new apparatus through which collectively to achieve their best interests. The search for these forms may take the believer anywhere, including the West. "Wisdom," Qaradawi quotes from a *hadith*, "is the lost property of the believer; wherever he discovers it, he has the best right to it." Fourth, since the first battle facing the Islamic resurgence in our time is the battle for freedom, Qaradawi would "join others to demand democracy as the most secure available means to achieve our aim of an honorable life, a life in which we can call for Islam and work for Allah without being thrown into the darkness of imprisonment or being strung from the hangman's scaffolding." Qaradawi concludes, "Hence, Islamic *shura* approaches the spirit of democracy, or if you will, the spirit of democracy approaches the spirit of Islamic *shura*."[44] In another context, Qaradawi expresses his preference for a multiparty system as long as there is a collective benefit or interest (*maslaha*, one of the principles of Islamic legislative interpretation) and as long as the multiparty framework is consonant with religious values and moral ideals.[45]

The ideas of Ghazali, Ghannouchi, Qaradawi, and other intellectuals have been endorsed by moderate Islamist movements in Egypt, Jordan, Tunisia, Yemen, Kuwait, Algeria, and other countries. Overall, the "Islamic mainstream has come to accept crucial elements of political democracy: pluralism (within the framework of Islam), political participation, government accountability, the rule of law and the protection of human rights."[46] For instance, the International Organization of the Muslim Brotherhood, an umbrella organization consisting of Islamic groups in several Arab countries with Egyptian Ikhwan dominating the leadership, released a statement in March 1994 supporting the gist of these scholars' arguments. "We believe in the existence of multiple political parties in the Islamic society," the statement declares, "and the authorities ought not restrict the formation of political parties and groups as long as the *shari`a* is the supreme constitution. . . . The recognition of multiple political parties entails the consent to a peaceful transfer of power between political groups and parties by means of periodic elections."[47]

Islamist thought is very much "thought in progress . . . activist, mobilizing thought, shaped and influenced by a political environment that in virtually all cases is neither liberal nor genuinely pluralistic, let alone democratic."[48] The position of moderate Islamist groups toward the limited democratization experiments in the Arab world has been supportive. On the level of practice, these groups have taken any opportunity to participate in elections. As Table 4.2 shows, Islamists have done better than predicted in political analyses produced by the ruling establishments and academic circles.

To sum up, Islamic resurgence movements, radicals and moderates alike, no matter what other issues they may disagree upon, all have this in common: They want to shift people's frame of reference toward Islam. They want to make Islam, with its diverse interpretations, the center of Muslim people's sense of self. Without denying the value of other overlapping kinds of identities, Islamists say, in effect, "Let Muslims be Muslims. Let us express our values in our public as well as private lives." This emerges from the perception that Muslims have not been allowed to "be Muslims," rather than a feeling that other religious groups should not have a respected place in Arab countries. Another common theme among Islamists is the need to develop Arab society by deriving solutions "from Islam." A prerequisite for achieving development, Islamists agree, is the creation of an Islamic political order, a state, that can ensure the widening of political participation and a

TABLE 4.2 Islamist Groups' Performance in Elections, 1985–1995

Country	*Election Type*	*Year*	*Islamic Participants*	*Rank*
Sudan	Parliament	1986	Islamic National Front	Third
Kuwait	National Assembly	1985	Islamists*	N. A.
	National Assembly	1992	Islamists	First
Egypt	Parliament**	1987	Islamic Alliance***	Second
Tunisia	Parliament**	1989	Al-Nahda	Second
Jordan	Parliament	1989	Botherhood; Independents	First
	Parliament	1993	Islamic Action Front	Second****
Algeria	Local & reg.	1990	FIS	First
	Parliament	1991	FIS	First
	Presidential	1995	Hamas	Second
Yemen	Parliament (North)	1988	Islamists*	N. A.
	Parliament	1993	Al-Islah	Second

Notes: *No recognized parties, but the Muslim Brotherhood (al-Islah) dominates here.

**The pro-government forces came in first; however, the IAF was first among the rest of the recognized political parties.

***Composed of the Muslim Brotherhood, the Labor Party, and the Liberal Party.

****Election fraud reported. Subsequent parliamentary elections took place in both Egypt (1990 and 1995) and Tunisia (1994). Elections were rigged and Islamists excluded.

Sources: Compiled from *Keesing's Record of World Events,* Vols. 31–41, 1985–1995; *The Middle East and North Africa,* 39th ed. (London: Europa Publications Ltd., 1992).

fairer distribution of resources. According to one Islamist, these two tasks are inseparable and must go hand in hand: "Development will bring out an Islamic pride in asserting our cultural identity and practicing our faith."[49]

Islamists have varied in the way they are pursuing their goals. While some of them—still in the minority—have resorted to radical methods, including the use of violence, the mainstream has advocated gradual and peaceful steps. The latter have taken advantage of democratic openings. They have contested and won in those elections in which they were allowed and seem to be making progress toward their objectives.

The problem, however, is that other forces, particularly ruling elites and secularists, have been seriously challenged by both radical and moderate Islamists. On one hand, Islamists' demands do constitute a challenge, if not a threat, to the state and the privileged elites in almost all Arab countries. Thus, Arab regimes have to struggle with these two aspects of the challenges posed by Islamists using a variety of tactics, ranging from co-optation to outright repression. Those regimes which allowed some openings decided to slow the democratization process, if not reverse course entirely, due to Islamist success. This is because Islamists enter the collective identity dynamic with a contesting proposal, one which is connected to the enfranchisement of currently marginalized people.

On the other hand, blaming Islamists for the democratization impasse is a mistake. It is not Islamists who have blocked democracy in the Arab world. How the struggle over the role of political Islam manifests itself and affects the democratic process is the subject of the next section.

Notes

1. Muhammad Shawqi Zaki, *Al-Ikhwan al-Muslimun wal Mujtama` al-Masri* (The Muslim Brotherhood and Egyptian Society)(Cairo: n.p., 1954).

2. Hasan al-Banna, *Majmu`at Rasa'il al-Imam al-Shahid Hasan al-Banna* (The Collected Letters of the Martyred Imam Hasan al-Banna) (Beirut: Al-Mu'assassa al-Islamiyya, 1981), p. 121.

3. Ishak Musa Hussaini, *The Muslim Brethren: The Greatest of Modern Islamic Movements* (Beirut: Khayat's College Book Cooperative, 1956), p. 68.

4. Hasan al-Banna, *Six Tracts of Hasan al-Banna* (Kuwait: International Islamic Federation of Student Organizations, n.d.), p. 63.

5. See for example two books by Kamel al-Sharif, *Al-Ikhwan al-Muslimun fi Harb Philistine* (The Muslim Brotherhood in the Palestine War) (Cairo: Maktabat Wahba, n.d.); and *Al-Muqawama as-Sirriyya fi Qanat as-Suwais 1951–1954* (The Secret Resistance in the Suez Canal 1951–1954)(Beirut: n.p., 1957).

6. Arab regimes called the 1967 war a mere *"naksa"* (setback). This term was perceived quite cynically by the Arab masses, who understood the depth of the catastrophe.

7. *A History of the Arab Peoples* (Cambridge, MA: Harvard University Press, 1989), p. 422.

8. Ibid., p. 423.

9. On the impact of 1967 on the issue of identity, see Yvonne Haddad, "The Arab-Israeli Wars, Nasserism, and the Affirmation of Islamic Identity," in John Esposito, ed., *Islam and Development* (Syracuse, NY: Syracuse University Press, 1980), pp. 107–121.

10. *The Arab World*, (Berkeley, CA: University of California Press, 1993), p. 169.

11. Mohammed Shaalan, "Political-Psychological Influences in Islamic Revivalist Movements," *Political Psychology*, Vol. 7, No.4, 1986, p. 815.

12. "Presidential Address 1989. The Study of Islam: Challenges and Prospects," *MESA Bulletin*, Vol. 24, 1990, p. 2.

13. Abdulwahab El-Affendi, *Turabi's Revolution: Islam and Power in Sudan* (London: Grey Seal Books, 1991), p. 1.

14. John Esposito, *The Islamic Threat: Myth or Reality?* (Oxford: Oxford University Press, 1992), p. 76.

15. The crisis, although not the *fatwa*, is summarized in Umar F. Abd-Allah, *The Islamic Struggle in Syria* (Berkeley, CA: Mizan Press, 1983), pp. 110–111.

16. Esposito, *The Islamic Threat*, p. 423.

17. This section is based in part on personal interviews with Islamists.

18. "Islam, Democracy, and the West," *Foreign Affairs*, Vol. 71, No. 3, 1992, p. 131.

19. "Al-Itar al-`Am lil Sahwa al-Islamiyya al-Mu`asera" (The General Framework of the Contemporary Islamic Resurgence) in Saad Eddin Ibrahim, ed., *Al-Sahwa al-Islamiyya wa Humum al-Watan al- `Arabi* (The Islamic Resurgence and the Concerns of the Arab World) (Amman: Muntada al-Fikr al-`Arabi, 1988), p. 65.

20. Rafa`t Said Ahmed, *Limaza Qatalu al-Sadat: Qisat Tanzim al-Jihad* (Why They Killed Sadat: The Story of the Al-Jihad Organization) (Cairo: Al-Dar al-Sharqiyya, 1989) and "Al-Islamiyyun: Al-Sulta wal `Unf (Islamists: Power and Violence), *Middle East Affairs Journal*, Vol. 2, No. 1, 1994, pp. 79–80.

21. Faraj's tract is included as an appendix in Ni`mallah Junaina, *Tanzim al-Jihad* (Al-Jihad Organization) (Cairo: Dar al-Huriyya, 1988), p. 246.

22. Based on the testimony of Jihad members who were brought to trial for the assassination of Sadat.

23. Junaina, *Tanzim al-Jihad*, p. 142.

24. "Egypt's Islamic Militants," *MERIP Reports*, February 1982, p. 11.

25. Personal interview with Muhammad Qutb, Makkah, Dec. 13, 1992. For elaboration on the Qutb school see Sayyid Qutb, *Ma`alim fil Tariq* (Milestones on the Path) (Cairo: Dar al-Shuruq, 1980) and Muhammad Qutb, *Jahiliyyat al-Qarn al-`Ishrin* (The Twentieth Century Ignorance) (Beirut: Dar al-Shuruq, 1978).

26. Personal interview, ibid.

27. Abd al-Mun`im M. Halima, (Amman: Al-Sharika al-Jadida, 1993), p. 40.

28. The main objective of the war, in the opinion of a majority of Islamists, was to destroy Iraq's capabilities.

29. See for example, *Muhakamat al-Nizam al-Siyasi* (Trials of the Political System), a tract published by al-Gama`a al-Islamiyya in Cairo, n.d.

30. *Al-Farida al-Gha'iba* (The Forgotten Obligation). In Junainah, *Tanzim al-Jihad*, p. 224.

31. Personal interview with Huwaidi in Cairo, Aug. 15, 1993. See also his article, "Al-Islam wal-Dimoqratiyya" (Islam and Democracy), *Al-Mustaqbal al-`Arabi*, No. 166, December, 1992.

32. *Al-Huriyat al-`Amma fil Dawla al-Islamiyya* (Public Liberties in the Islamic State) (Beirut: Markaz Dirasat al-Wahda al-`Arabia, 1993), p. 224.

33. Wright, "Islam, Democracy . . . ," p. 132.

34. Including: Egyptian *ulama* Muhammad al-Ghazali and Yusuf al- Qaradawi; independent Islamist writers Fahmi Huwaidi, Tawfiq al-Shawi, Muhammad `Amara, Tariq al-Bishri, and Muhammad Salim el-`Awa; Rashid al-Ghannouchi, Hasan al-Turabi, and Ishaq al-Farhan, leaders of Islamic organizations in Tunisia, Sudan, and Jordan, respectively.

35. One of many conferences among Islamists on this issue was held in Cairo in 1992 on "Al-Ta`adudiyya al-Siasiyya fil Islam" (Political Pluralism in Islam), in which major Islamist scholars espoused the concept of pluralism.

36. Gudrun Kramer, "Islamist Notions of Democracy," *Middle East Report*, July-August 1993, p. 8.

37. One of Ghazali's early works is *Al-Islam wal Istibdad al- Siyasi* (Islam and Political Despotism) (Cairo: Dar al-Kitab al-`Arabi, 1949), a telling example of his attack on authoritarian rule.

38. Ghannouchi wrote it as a Ph.D. dissertation while in prison from 1981 to 1984 and then in hiding in 1986. It was published in 1993.

39. *Al-Huriyat al-`Amma*, p. 88.

40. Ibid., p. 133.

41. Ibid., p. 297.

42. Ibid., p. 316.

43. Personal interview, Cairo, Aug. 13, 1993. See also his book *Fatawa Mu`asira* (Contemporary *Fatwas*) (Cairo: Dar al-Wafa', 1993), Vol. 2.

44. Ibid., p. 651.

45. Ibid., p. 660.

46. Kramer, "Islamist Notions of Democracy," p. 8.

47. "Mujaz `An al-Shura fil Islam wa Ta`adud al-Ahzab fil Mujtama` al-Muslim" (A Brief on Consultation in Islam and Party Pluralism in Muslim Society), *Resolutions and Recommendations Issued by the International Organization of the Muslim Brotherhood*. Pamphlet, March 1994, p. 3.

48. Kramer, "Islamist Notions of Democracy," p. 8.

49. Rachid Ben Eissa, "The Algerian Experiment," in Azzam Tamimi, ed., *Power-Sharing Islam?* (London: Liberty for Muslim World Publications, 1993), p. 143.

PART THREE

The Politics of Inclusion and Exclusion: Two Case Studies

5

Egypt: Coercion and Containment

Democratization in Egypt has fluctuated over the past two decades with the regime's efforts to contain the Islamist challenge. Since the mid-1970s, Islamists have been the most popular force opposing the ruling order. Islamists have used the modest increases in the margin of freedom granted by the regime and its occasional tolerance toward the moderate element of the Islamic movement to make gains. The regime, on its part, has been determined to exclude Islamists from political participation. Exclusion has been accomplished by a combination of coercion and containment. That is, the state uses its repressive apparatus to try to eradicate radical Islamists while allowing mainstream Islamists to function, but within constraints that preclude their political participation. The policy of excluding Islamists has led those who rule Egypt to retreat from democratization. This is more than just a move by a ruling group to preserve its privilege and keep one more group of contenders away from power. In the policies of the Egyptian government toward Islamists there is an outraged objection to the very idea of an "Islamic solution" that seems to brook no compromise. This points to sharp disagreement over the contours of collective identity.

The socioeconomic context for this conflict is that Egypt has poor resources and a huge population. The tiny ruling strata holds tightly to these limited resources. Meanwhile, the Islamist crowds are beating at the door demanding their share. The international context further exacerbates the divide. Because Egypt is not a marginal Arab state but a key ally for the United States and European powers, these powers lend their weight to make sure the ruling group stays in control. All these factors further polarize the conflict over who is to be included or excluded in the political process in Egypt. These factors shape the politics of democratization in Egypt.

How do democratic development and the rise of Islamists intersect in Egypt? How did Egypt arrive at the stalemate of the 1990s which has produced such violent political confrontation in that country? Is there any solid ground upon which democratization in Egypt could develop?

Democratic Development in Egypt, 1970–1990

Egypt, in the post-Nasser decades, has gradually shifted from a one-party authoritarian state with complete control of the People's Assembly and the press to a cautiously multiparty authoritarian state with more meaningful elections, a moderate margin of freedom of the press, and wary tolerance of some oppositional politics. On one hand, the very existence of the Ikhwan (the Muslim Brotherhood) and other groups advocating an "Islamic" political order is tolerated in Egypt as it is not, for example, in Syria. Proselytizing and other Islamist social and cultural activities which the government perceives as nonthreatening are permitted, for the most part. On the other hand, tolerance is not the same as inclusion. The regime maintains close watch on Islamist activities. If Islamist organizations step over a certain line, arbitrarily defined by the government and constantly shifting, they are targeted for suppression. Such "tolerance" is carefully measured by the Egyptian regime so as to exclude the major opposition movement, that of moderate Islamists, from direct participation in politics. Government policy is also designed to prevent them from gaining whatever is deemed as too much economic strength, leverage in professional institutions and unions, and influence in the media.

Anwar Sadat's takeover after Gamal Abdul Nasser's death marked a dramatic shift in Egypt's domestic policy and foreign orientation. Sadat, who was Nasser's last Vice President, was confirmed as President in a public referendum. After a brief power struggle, Sadat consolidated his control, dismissing Vice President Ali Sabri and left-leaning party figures. Although it did not appear so to the world until after the 1973 war, a leader with an agenda very different from Nasser's had come to govern Egypt.

Sadat introduced some measure of political and economic liberalization. He released hundreds of members of the Egyptian Muslim Brotherhood and political prisoners of various persuasions, allowing them to resume some of their proselytizing activities.[1] He also introduced a range of economic reforms. In 1974, Sadat officially replaced Nasser's socialist planning with an *infitah* (Open Door) policy, emphasizing reconstruction, encouraging foreign investment, and introducing a private enterprise sector.[2] However, because reforms benefitted a very small business elite, widening the gap between rich and poor classes and exposing the inability of government policies to meet the needs of the lower classes,[3] *infitah* provided grist for Sadat's political opposition. Islamists responded to the conditions created by *infitah* by providing economic assistance to the masses left outside the "open door."

Second, Sadat committed himself to finding a peaceful solution to the Arab-Israeli conflict. He believed that Egypt's participation in the 1973 war was the only way to break a stalemate which had stalled the peace process. The War thus ironically moved the parties closer to negotiation.[4] Third, he turned from reliance on the Soviet Union for weapons and political support, moving his country closer to the United States and the West in general.[5] Finally, Sadat moved away from Nasser's Arab nationalism toward Egyptianism, changing the official name of the country from the United Arab Republic to the Arab Republic of Egypt. Sadat did not totally abandon the idea of Arabism,[6] but believed in "Egypt first," which found a certain following among the Egyptian people. When he opted for a separate peace in the Arab-Israeli conflict, he justified it partly in terms of Egypt's economic imperative: The country could not afford another war with Israel. In 1978 when the other Arab countries, in a Baghdad summit, offered to compensate for Egypt's promised foreign aid from the West on the condition that he abandon negotiation for a separate treaty with Israel, Sadat turned down the offer. He was ready to accept isolation from the Arab world if that meant prosperity and peace for Egypt. Sadat carried this orientation to an extreme which provoked domestic opposition, especially from Nationalists and Islamists, who perceived Sadat's foreign policy as a sell-out to the West. The "prosperity" Sadat touted never came for the Egyptian masses; the profits which were to be the trade-off for Egypt's ostracism by other Arab states accrued to a tiny business elite. Islamist social work thus continued to find a constituency whose needs remained unmet by the state.

Sadat, lacking the charisma of Nasser, needed to begin his rule with political liberalization to establish a measure of legitimacy that could sustain him through his deviation from Nasserite policy. An important change during his tenure was the gradual end of one-party rule between 1976 and 1978. Sadat wanted to legalize political parties, yet without allowing the opposition too much power. He first permitted the formation of three groups within the Arab Socialist Union, which soon developed into three political parties. He set strict rules for the formation of political parties in 1977, by which he prevented the revival of the Wafd party and suspended one of three groups initially allowed (the National Progressive Unionist Party). In 1977, Sadat announced the creation of a new political party, the National Democratic Party, under his chairmanship. A year later he allowed the formation of the Socialist Labor Party (SLP) as the official opposition party.[7] He made sure to strengthen his authority, however, by pushing through a new constitution vesting executive power in the president, who was to be nominated by the People's Assembly and elected for a six-year term by popular referendum. The president was to appoint a council of ministers and could rule by decree when granted emergency power by the parliament (People's Assembly). The Assembly would function as a rubber-stamping rather than policy-making body.[8]

Despite the Open Door economic program, political liberalization, and the peace with Israel, Sadat's government faced growing opposition. For instance, in January 1977, when food prices shot up after the removal of price subsidies, intense riots broke out all over Egypt. The government had to revoke the price increases and introduce a variety of legal measures to prevent the recurrence of such riots. Discontent in 1980 increased over economic hardship and misgovernment, as well as out of increasing opposition to the treaty with Israel and the concomitant isolation of Egypt from the rest of the Arab world. In the summer of 1981, after an increase in sectarian strife between Muslims and Copts, Sadat ordered a crackdown on the opposition. His security forces arrested more than 1,000 opposition figures of all persuasions, including Islamists, Nasserites, and Communists; Copts as well as Muslims were rounded up. He placed Egypt's 40,000 privately operated mosques under government control.[9] It was obvious that Sadat had unleashed forces he was no longer able to control except by reverting to coercion and repression. Like Mikhail Gorbachev, Sadat became the victim of his own liberalizing actions. Unlike the Soviet leader, however, Sadat attempted to turn back the tide which his own liberalization had released. His crackdown on all opposition figures and his caustic words against them enraged many Egyptians. It was a small militant Islamist group, al-Jihad, which translated that rage into action. On October 6, 1981, while attending the annual military parade celebrating the 1973 "victory," Sadat was assassinated by members of Jihad.[10] One week later, Husni Mubarak, Sadat's Vice President, was confirmed as President in a national referendum. Mubarak's reign has been similar to that of Sadat. He began his rule with political opening, cultivated in two parliamentary elections in 1984 and 1987, as well as an achievement in foreign policy, restoring Egypt's relations with all Arab countries. Then, like Sadat, he reverted more and more to authoritarian tactics toward the end of his first decade in power. As under Sadat, economic conditions have not improved, and the Islamist challenge has not eroded. On the contrary, the government's performance has deteriorated and challenge from radical Islamists has intensified; the country has entered a period of escalating violence in the 1990s.

How much democratic opening has really occurred under Mubarak? The regime never discarded the use of coercive measures, even when some liberalizing steps were introduced. The regime has introduced some openings only as a way to preserve its hold on power. And most of the democratic steps adopted during Mubarak's rule have been superficial, as the following survey of events from 1981 to 1990 will show.[11]

The government released most oppositional figures who had been jailed in the summer of 1981. In 1984, 174 of the 302 people arrested in conjunction with Sadat's killing for plotting to overthrow the government were acquitted. Yet the state of emergency imposed after the assassination of Sadat was extended again and again (and is still in force). The government also continued its sweep of arrests of radical Islamists.

In early 1984, the government legalized an important opposition party, the New Wafd. In the same year, the first election of the People's Assembly under Mubarak took place. However, electoral law required parties to receive a minimum of 8 percent of the total vote to be represented in the Assembly. The only party able to cross this threshold was the New Wafd, which had allowed the Muslim Brotherhood candidates to run on its lists. In this election the New Wafd, despite reported government fraud, won 15.8 percent of the vote (see Table 5.1). Mubarak held this election not out of commitment to democratic reform, but so that "he could consolidate his authority and at the same time (by restoring a measure of real democracy) establish himself as a popular leader, tolerant, within limits, of opposition . . . "[12]

The second election for the People's Assembly to occur during Mubarak's term took place in 1987 after a ruling by the Supreme Constitutional Court that the previous election in 1984 was unconstitutional because it had not allowed independent candidates to stand for election. But the immediate reasons for holding the election were the riots which erupted in the South, led by Islamic radicals protesting the government's ban against veiled women on campus, and an earlier report about a coup plot involving Islamists. Mubarak wanted to secure a second term as president and needed to claim a mandate from a wide segment of the population. In this election, Mubarak's National Democratic Party maintained its dominance in the new assembly, but a new coalition of two parties (the Socialist Labor Party and the Liberal Party) with the Ikhwan (Muslim Brotherhood) emerged as the largest opposition bloc. The coalition, calling itself the Islamic Alliance, won a total of 60 seats, of which the Ikhwan had 37. The New Wafd won only 35 seats, down from 50 in 1984, and independent candidates mostly affiliated with the ruling party filled the 48 seats provided by the new electoral law (see Table 5.2).

The 1987 election, despite widespread government fraud and intimidation,[13] was significant because it increased the representation of the opposition substantially compared to previous elections. The emergence of the Ikhwan as the largest opposition group, even without legal recognition, startled the ruling elite and precipitated its decision to slow down the democratic experiment and revert to more authoritarian practices. Meanwhile (in July 1987), Mubarak was nominated by a two-thirds

TABLE 5.1 The Results of the 1984 People's Assembly Election

Party	*Seats*	*Percent of Votes*
National Democratic	384	72.9
New Wafd	58*	15.8
Socialist Labor	—	7.1
National Progressive Unionist	—	4.2
Liberal Socialist	—	0.6
Total	448	100

Note: *The Ikhwan's share was eight seats.

Sources: "Egypt," *The Middle East and North Africa 1984–1985,* 31st ed. (London: Europa Publications Ltd., 1984), p. 342; Mona Makram Ebeid, "The Role of Official Opposition," in Charles Tripp and Roger Owen, eds., *Egypt Under Mubarak* (London: Routledge, 1987), p. 41.

TABLE 5.2 The Results of the 1987 People's Assembly Election

Party	*Seats*	*Percent of Votes*
National Democratic	346	69.3
Islamic Alliance*	60	17.0
New Wafd	35	10.9
National Progressive Unionist**	—	—
Umma**	—	—
Independent	7***	—
Total	448	100

Notes: *The Ikhwan's share was thirty-seven seats.

**These parties failed to win the minimum of 8 percent of total votes required for representation in the Assembly and their votes were transfered to the NDP.

***The total number given to independents, according to the new electoral law, was forty-eight, but forty-one of them were affiliated with NDP.

Sources: "Egypt," *The Middle East and North Africa 1988,* 34st ed. (London: Europa Publications Ltd., 1987), p. 368; Mona Makram Ebeid, "The Role of Official Opposition," in Charles Tripp and Roger Owen, eds., *Egypt Under Mubarak* (London: Routledge, 1987), p. 41.

majority of the Assembly and confirmed for a second term by a national referendum, by an alleged 97.1 percent of votes cast.

As unrest continued through 1988–89, the government responded with more arrests, particularly during the holy month of Ramadan 1989. Most of the detainees were identified as Islamists. A month later, the elections for the Shura Council (the upper house created in 1980) were held. This was the first time the opposition parties were allowed to contest. The Islamic Alliance contested, while the New Wafd party boycotted the election. The first sign of the regime's intention to abort the democratic project were election returns, in which the ruling party "won" all the contested seats. It was widely believed that the government rigged the election.[14] Government efforts to prevent the representation of any opposition member to the Shura Council left bitterness among Islamic Alliance candidates. It was the Shura election which led the opposition, and the Ikhwan in particular, to question the virtue of participation and to hesitate before running in future elections without minimum guarantees of fairness.[15]

In 1990 there were three positive developments related to the struggle for democracy. The first was the dismissal of the Minister of the Interior, Zaki Badr. Badr was the ugly face of the regime. Not only had he conducted the ruthless campaign against the Islamic radicals, but he also harassed and confronted most of the opposition. On January 9, 1990, the opposition newspaper *al-Sha`b* published on the first page a transcript of a speech he had delivered accusing opposition and prominent intellectuals of treason, and cursing them in vulgar language.[16] All oppositional parties, along with journalists and intellectuals, organized a campaign against the Minister. Badr's dismissal was considered a victory for the opposition.

The second development was more symbolic than substantive. The government legalized three new political parties, bringing the total number to nine. However, these new parties, the Green Party, the Democratic Unionist, and the Young Egypt, were distinctly lacking in popular bases.

The third development was the Supreme Constitutional Court's ruling in May 1990 that the 1987 Assembly elections were unconstitutional because electoral laws had discriminated against independent candidates. The government responded by calling for a referendum about whether to dissolve the Assembly or not. A majority of those who participated in the referendum supported the dissolution of the Assembly; it was dissolved on October 12. This set the stage for a new election. Electoral laws were amended by the government so that the 8 percent threshold was removed. The party list system was abolished and all candidates had to run as independents. While the main opposition parties welcomed the dissolution of the Assembly and were ready to participate in the new election, they boycotted the election because the government refused to guarantee judicial, instead of police, supervision of the election, and to repeal emergency laws. Only the left-oriented National Progressive Unionist Party (NPUP) broke from the agreement reached by leaders of Wafd, Labor, Liberals, and Ikhwan. The NPUP, despite its skepticism about the government's honesty, saw an opportunity to win seats in the absence of real competition with the more popular parties.[17] The ruling party, of course, won the majority of seats (see Table 5.3).

TABLE 5.3 The Results of the 1990 People's Assembly Election

Party	*Seats*	*Percent of Votes*
National Democratic	348	79.6
National Progressive Unionist	6	1.4
Independents	83*	19.0
Total	437**	100

Notes: *Of the eighty-three independents, fifty-six were affiliated with the NDP, fourteen with the New Wafd, eight with the SLP, and one with the SP.
**Voting was suspended in three constituencies and for one seat of the fourth.
Sources: Mahmud Akef and Muhammed Ghurab, *al-umma fi Am (The Nation in One Year)* (Cairo: Umma Press & al-istishariyyun al-`Arab, 1991), p. 42, and "Egypt," *The Middle East and North Africa 1993*, 39th ed. (London: Europa Publications Ltd., 1993), pp. 396 and 374.

Three remarks about the 1990 election are in order. First, despite the decision of the major opposition parties (the New Wafd, Labor, and the Liberals) to boycott the election, some of their followers did not abide by the party decision. These defectors were encouraged by the government to give the election some credibility; however, most of these candidates were suspended by their parties. Second, having anticipated no serious competition, the government had allowed a higher degree of fairness and minimized police interference in the election proceedings.[18] Nevertheless, the boycott affected the election by discouraging voter turnout. Even according to governmental sources, only 19 percent of those eligible voted in the election. In some constituencies, especially in Cairo, the turnout was around 7 percent.[19] Finally, government refusal to accommodate opposition demands for guarantees of fairness undermined the credibility of the election. The refusal to provide mechanisms for ensuring fair elections has increased apathy among Egyptian people, especially the young and marginalized, many of whom expressed their dissatisfaction by turning to Islamic sources for a critique of the regime.

In foreign policy, Mubarak succeeded in balancing Egypt's peace requirements with Israel, maintaining strong relations with the US, and restoring diplomatic relations with all the Arab countries. The Egyptian government was able to regain the Sinai peninsula from Israel despite constraints in the relations between the two countries, which reached a low point after the Israeli invasion of Lebanon. Egypt under Mubarak managed to remain a major ally of the US in the area. This alliance has brought American military and economic assistance to Egypt. Egypt, in turn, has acted in accordance with US interest in the region, as manifesting in its joining the US-led alliance against Iraq in the Gulf War. The skill of Egyptian diplomacy lay in pursuing Egyptian interests with both Israel and the US, while restoring the country's good relations within the Arab world. Egypt had made a comeback as a major player in the Arab world by the end of 1989. In 1990, Arab League headquarters was moved from Tunis back to Cairo. These achievements, however, neither impressed Mubarak's opposition nor improved the conditions of the average Egyptian.

The Islamist Challenge in Egypt

Since the 1980s, the Islamist movement has constituted the main political challenge to the Egyptian state, in two ways. Radical Islamist groups pose a security threat to the state. More significantly, moderate Islamists, who have steadily built a popular base, developed institutions, and begun to negotiate a space for themselves in the political process, pose the threat of an eventual transfer of power, of major change in the established order. The government has responded to the first threat by simple repressive measures. Regarding the second threat, the state has oscillated between coercive measures and co-optive tolerance intended to minimize the role of Islamists in politics. Unlike the Jordanian state, the Egyptian government has not considered inclusion of Islamists within the political process as a viable option.

The Islamic trend in Egypt has several manifestations. One is the increased signs of religious observance among the Egyptian people in the last two decades. Another is the fact that almost all political parties, to varying degrees, have accepted the central role of Islam as a source of identity and a frame of reference. In the 1987 parliamentary election, all political parties, from right to left, including the NDP, (the ruling party) included in their campaigns a commitment to implement *shari`a* (Islamic law).[20] Even the ruling elite and its party quickly understood the necessity of using Islam to legitimize its rule. The manipulation of "Islam" by the state began immediately after Sadat took over. Not only did he release hundreds of the Ikhwan, but he allowed them to propagate their brand of Islam in a new order, calling himself "the believing President." In 1980, he affirmed Egypt's adherence to Islamic jurisprudence by an amendment making *shari`a* the main source of legislation.[21] Of course, Sadat's use of Islam backfired on him, as it encouraged radical Islamists to judge and ultimately indict him by what they believed to be Islamic standards.

The most salient manifestation of the Islamist trend is the burgeoning of various groups which are striving to move Egypt toward their vision of an Islamic order. These groups are of two distinct kinds: the radical militant groups and the mainstream or moderate Islamic ones, particularly the Ikhwan.

The Radical Groups

It is estimated today that the number of these groups (*gama`at*) is around twenty. Most scholars of contemporary Egypt agree that the origins of these groups can be traced to the last few years of Nasser's rule. The brutal tortures inflicted on Islamists led many of them to question whether the people in the regime were actually Muslims like themselves. The intellectual basis for many of these radicals is their reading of Sayed Qutb in *Ma`alim fil Tariq* (Milestones). In this book, Qutb distinguishes between Islamic rule deriving its authority from God, and *jahiliyya* (ignorance), which includes all other rules—nationalist, capitalist, communist, and others.[22] The radical groups which emerged in the seventies and 1980s carried Qutb's argument a step further. For them, the regimes which control most Arab and Muslim nations fall into the *jahiliyya* or unbelief category and are therefore illegitimate. The struggle to overthrow such regimes is a religious duty. It is a struggle between right and wrong, faith and unbelief.[23] Members of these groups have attempted to overthrow the existing order, carrying attacks against various targets associated with the regime. Here are examples of acts of violence by radical Islamist groups:[24]

1. In 1974, a small group calling itself Gama`at al-Tahrir al-Islami (the Islamic Liberation Group) carried out an attempt to seize the Military Technical School in order to topple the regime. The attempt failed and the leader of the group, Dr. Salih Siriyya, was executed.
2. Another group, Gama`at al-Muslimin (the Group of Muslims) known popularly as al-Takfir wal Hijra (Excommunication and Emigration) abducted a former Minister of Religious Affairs in 1977. The group demanded the release of some of their members as a condition for the release of its hostage. The operation ended with the killing of the hostage and the capture of the group's leaders, four of whom were executed in the same year.
3. A newly formed group, al-Jihad, decided to organize a revolt against the Sadat regime in October 1981. Only the first part of the plot, the assassination of Sadat, was successful. While five of the assassins were executed shortly thereafter, around three hundred members were tried in 1984. Of them, 174 were convicted, receiving prison sentences ranging from two years to life. This group and its offshoot, Tala'e` al-Fath (Vanguard of Conquest, or the New Jihad) and its rival, al-Gama`a al- Islamiyya (the Islamic Group) are the two principal radical Islamic organizations in Egypt today.

It is widely believed even by sources close to the government that the conditions in Egypt under Mubarak's regime constituted a suitable environment for the proliferation of such groups. Among these conditions are: extreme poverty, high unemployment, lack of meaningful avenues for political participation, and the widening gap between the rich and poor. Members of society who despair of ever gaining a stake in the system or a voice in its decision-making process are most likely to become radical or revolutionary. In addition, the extreme cruelty with which the regime has dealt with followers of these groups has generated counter-violence and terrorism. To the regime, these groups constitute a security threat and should be treated as such.

Moderate Movements

Moderate Islamists include the durable Ikhwan (established in 1927 by Hasan al-Banna) as well as a loose cluster of other groups and individuals who believe in the gradual Islamic reform of society and state. Of all the oppositional parties, legal and illegal, the Ikhwan has been the most popular movement under both Sadat and Mubarak. As detailed in Chapter Four, the Ikhwan had enjoyed a measure of popularity before Nasser. Despite initial Ikhwan support for Nasser's revolution, the movement came into conflict with him. Nasser was successful in utilizing the power of the state, particularly coercion and propaganda, to suppress the Ikhwan. After their release from prison in the early seventies, surviving movement leaders, most of whom had spent at least ten years in prison, embarked on a very cautious and moderate approach in dealing with the political order. For the most part, they were accommodating and acquiescent in dealing with the Sadat regime. Their hard experience with Nasser led them to reject violence and to work gradually, concentrating on society rather than the state as an arena for transformation. Toward the end of Sadat's years, they became more critical of some of his policies, especially *infitah* (the economic "Open Door" policy) which created a small class of beneficiaries and raised the masses' expectations without being able to satisfy them. The second area of disagreement with Sadat was over the signing of a separate deal with Israel. Hence, their leaders were included in the arrest campaign in the summer of 1981, which targeted all opposition figures.

It was reportedly during this imprisonment that the leader of Ikhwan, Umar al-Talmasani, and the leader of the New Wafd, Fu'ad Siraj al-Din, were able to debate a few issues and lay down the grounds for the alliance between the two groups in 1984. This alliance enabled the Ikhwan to contest that year's election and win eight seats. While the Ikhwan was making a political comeback through the parliament, it continued to work to reform the individual and society through proselytizing and disseminating religious literature. Also, Ikhwan Islamists were increasingly involved in forming economic institutions independent of the state.

Several mainstream groups and respected intellectuals joined the ranks of moderate Islamists during the 1980s. Among the intellectual independents who made the conversion: Muhammad Amara, Tariq al-Bishri, and Adel Hussein. Also, among the main political movements which became more Islamic in its orientation was the Socialist Labor Party. According to its Assistant Secretary General, Magdi Qarqar, it was during the fourth general conference in January 1987 that the Party asserted its Arabic-Islamic identity and defined an Islamic agenda addressing society's problems.[25] This transformation brought Labor closer to the Ikhwan and the Liberal Party, eventually resulting in a coalition called the Islamic Alliance. The motto of the Alliance in the 1987 parliamentary election was "Islam is the Solution." The Islamization of the Party was not without problems. A small group, led by the vice president of the party, and with governmental encouragement, led a struggle inside the party to protest the takeover by pro-Islamist elements. While this led to a split within the party, its leaders adhered to the new Islamic orientation. Because members opposing the Islamist direction left, the Labor-Ikhwan alliance proved more durable than the alliance between the Ikhwan and the New Wafd. The Labor Party newspaper, *al-Sha`b*, has been a strong voice of opposition to Mubarak regime and an outlet for the leaders of the Ikhwan to express their views since they do not have a paper or magazine of their own.[26]

Having proven itself a viable partner in electoral politics, the Ikhwan became an attractive alliance party. In the second parliamentary election in 1987, the Ikhwan candidates dominated, winning thirty-seven seats out of sixty (the total share of the alliance). The Ikhwan became indisputably the main official opposition party in the country, without even being recognized as a legal political party. Through their coalition-building experiences with other opposition parties, the Ikhwan membership has learned how to function within a multiparty framework and has demonstrated a commitment to the rules of democratic participation. "No matter what the regime tries to do, there is only one solution to the crisis and only one way to a better future, and that is true and real democracy," declared an Ikhwan leader.[27]

The demands made by Ikhwan members serving in parliament reveal their moderate and reformist agenda. For example, they have called for the complete implementation of *shari`a* in compliance with the amendment to the constitution; an end to emergency laws and growth in the margin of freedom; change in the law which regulates the formation of parties, so they can form a political party of their own; Islamic alternatives to particular problems, such as usury (*riba*); reform of the educational system; and an end to the corruption and inertia of the bureaucracy.[28]

In short, the most important and most popular opposition group in Egypt, the Ikhwan, is a moderate organization which has indicated in word and deed its capacity and willingness to work within the system despite the legal and illegal constraints under which the government has put it. The Egyptian government has responded with harassment, intimidation, and determination to exclude the Ikhwan from meaningful participation in the political process.

The Democratization Stalemate in the 1990s

Mubarak's regime has, for the last two decades, employed a dual strategy of suppression of the radicals and co-optation of the moderates within a narrow margin of freedom. The year 1989–1990 was a turning point for democratization and Islamists, in which the state tried to turn back both these trends. The blatant government fraud in the 1989 Shura Council elections and the government's refusal to guarantee judicial supervision of the 1990 elections, marked the outer boundaries of the regime's political reform and liberalization. The regime has attempted to retract the margin of political freedom. The closing of the door of meaningful political participation against the moderate Islamists, the most viable opposition, has added to the regime's record of failure and corruption.

The first component of the state strategy directed at radical Islamists is one of harsh suppression. The government has used the emergency laws in effect since 1981, giving the security forces wideranging powers of arrest and detention. The campaign of detention has increased dramatically in response to the violent waves of attack by militant Islamists against government figures and security forces beginning in 1991. In one figure obtained from government sources, the number of detention orders between January 1991 and October 1993 reached 24,568 detainees whose detention time lasted between forty-five days to three years. Comparing the same figures of detainees with those under Nasser and Sadat shows a conspicuous increase in the reliance on this measure. The number of political detainees under Nasser and Sadat were 14,000 and 19,000 respectively.[29] According to many human rights organizations, the current government uses torture routinely. In the early 1990s, several people have died under torture. The most reported case was that of Abdel Hareth Madani, a lawyer known for his defense of militant Islamists. Madani was arrested on April 26, 1993; one week later, his family was asked to come and collect his body. The family's request for an autopsy was denied. This incident caused a major confrontation between the lawyers' union, dominated by moderate Ikhwan, and the government. More than one thousand lawyers demonstrated in protest of the torture of their colleague. The government used tear gas to disperse the demonstrators.[30]

In addition to the emergency laws, the government has relied on two additional measures. First, the parliament passed an antiterrorist law in July 1992 which makes membership in any organization defined as terrorist a crime punishable by death and further empowered the security forces to detain suspects without notifying the prosecutor's office. Second, after the trial of twenty-seven suspects for killing the former speaker of parliament in 1990, in which the civilian court found all of them not guilty,[31] the government has been using military courts to ensure the speedy trial and conviction of militant Islamists.[32] Since 1992, sixty Islamists have been sentenced to death.[33] In the few years since 1990, there have been more political executions in Egypt than under any other Egyptian regime this century.

Despite the government's insistence with every arrest that it has completely eliminated the "terrorists,"[34] political violence is far from over in Egypt. In fact, the available numbers show an increase in the number of people killed between 1992 and 1994. The total number of people killed reached ninety-four in 1992, 341 in 1993, and 234 as of October 1994. The victims of political violence have been civilians, militants, and security forces (see Table 5.4).

Militant Islamists have targeted security personnel, government officials, particularly the Interior Minister (there were assassination attempts on the life of almost every Interior Minister under Mubarak), Copts, anti-Islamist intellectuals, and lately foreign tourists. The government's intense security crackdown appears to be working. The fact that the militants lack resources, unity, and charismatic leadership,[35] coupled with excessive repression by the government, all have made the militants more of a security issue to the Mubarak regime than a true threat to political stability.[36]

The second component of the government's strategy to combat the Islamist challenge has been to contain and co-opt the rise of the moderate Ikhwan. As discussed earlier, the Ikhwan decided to utilize the margin of freedom provided by the government, entering the political process on the lists of other legalized parties (Wafd in 1984 and Labor and Liberal in 1987). While its participation was tolerated, relations between the Ikhwan and the Mubarak regime have been strained. The closest point of rapprochement with the government came after an unexpected Ikhwan victory in the parliamentary elections of 1987. In appreciation for what they took to be a sign of substantive change and a promise of genuine reform, the Ikhwan as well as most other parties endorsed Mubarak for a second term a few months later.

TABLE 5.4 Casualties of Political Violence in Egypt, 1993

Type of Casualty	*Killed*	*Wounded*
Security forces	120	181
Militant Islamists	111	252
Civilians	101	341
Total	341	774

Source: Compiled from *Civil Society*, Vols. 2 and 3, 1993–1994.

Nevertheless, the government never relaxed its campaign of arrest and intimidation against the Ikhwan, not even during that shortlived honeymoon of 1987–1988.[37] After 1990, Mubarak's regime decided to exclude the Ikhwan from the political process altogether. Mubarak was quoted in Arabic newspapers as having told former Algerian President Chazli Benjedid not to allow the Islamists to contest in a free election in Algeria. According to one Ikhwan leader, Mubarak "declared many times that he would not repeat the same mistake of granting the Islamists the right to officially engage in political activities or participate in democratic elections. So far, the Muslim Brotherhood, the largest Islamist group in Egypt, continues to be prevented from acting as a political party or officially forming one."[38] Mubarak's fears are not unrealistic. The outcome of the Algerian elections only strengthened his conviction that allowing free and fair elections would mean unseating his regime. In one recent report on Egypt, Robert Kaplan concludes that "the overwhelming majority of Egyptians and Western diplomats I asked said that if truly free elections were ever held in Egypt, the Muslim Brotherhood would probably win the most votes. That's as specific as the information gets."[39]

Having understood the regime's unwillingness to let the Ikhwan win in a free election, the Ikhwan has concentrated its energies on winning control of professional associations, unions, and charitable organizations. The Ikhwan uses its leadership in these organizations to do what the government has been increasingly unable to do: provide assistance to the lower strata of society who live in the slums of Cairo and upper Egypt (where the government is only visible through the police). Another dimension of the Ikhwan's role is in providing members of the professional associations under its leadership with affordable services. For example, the 80,000-member physicians' union led by the Ikhwan "gives physicians and their families the best quality health care at a minimal price. They have a reputation for being honest and careful with union funds. That reputation has wide appeal in a country whose government is seen as thoroughly corrupt."[40] As of 1993, the Ikhwan has been able to dominate, or at least do well in, the elected boards of the unions of doctors, pharmacists, engineers, and teachers; the association of university professors; student unions at Egypt's universities; and many of the 14,000 private philanthropies.[41] Louis Cantori, in his field research in Egypt, found in the area of Cairo and Alexandria alone around 9,000 charitable Islamic organizations providing welfare services, jobs, and education to the needy. Government-controlled mosques[42] and private mosques cooperate in running these institutions. In Egypt today, Cantori concludes, "there are Islamic infrastructure that protect and educate the masses."[43]

What became obvious in the early 1990s in Egypt is the decline of the state's ability to carry out its welfare functions. It was the Ikhwan and other Islamists who jumped to fill this vacuum. Although the work of the Ikhwan in this area contributes to the maintenance of social order, the government has repeatedly intervened in the affairs of these "independent" voluntary associations to assert its control and draw lines on what might be tolerated and what will not. Here are examples of such intervention:

1. In 1988, the government passed a law to organize the activities of the investment companies which proliferated in the mid-1980s. Many of these companies were run by Islamists and conducted according to Islamic economic principles. Although there was something dubious about a few of these companies because of the high profit rates they were claiming, the government was mostly alarmed by the willingness of so many people to trust Islamists with their life's savings and to contribute to the economic power of Islamists.[44]

2. In February 1992, security forces stormed a computer company, Salsabil, whose owners were known to be Islamists. The government charged the owners of plotting with the Ikhwan to overthrow the government. Although the company's activities were well-known to the government, which had even been a Salsabil client, the real fear was that Ikhwan members were becoming more skilled in the field of information-processing. Authoritarian regimes do not feel comfortable with opposition groups gaining this kind of expertise. Thus the government wanted to set limits on the expansion of Islamists in this area.[45]

3. After the victory of all sixteen Ikhwan candidates for the board of the 25-seat Lawyers' Syndicate, the government was alarmed by Islamist influence in one of the last strongholds of secular liberals and leftists. The government responded by issuing a new syndicate law in February 1993. The new law required a turnout of 50 percent of the syndicate members in the first round and 33 percent in the second round. Failing this, the government would appoint a council to run the syndicate.[46] The purpose

of this law was to reduce, if not eliminate, the influence of Ikhwan members in these syndicates.

Thus, on one hand, the lack of popular access to meaningful political participation, as well as the government's inability to fulfill some of its social and economic functions, have left spaces which have been filled for the most part by moderate Islamists. This stabilizing role is one the government cannot easily eliminate. On the other hand, the regime cannot and has not let Islamist influence go unchecked. One researcher has characterized the relationship between Egypt's authoritarian state and the parallel Islamic sphere as marked by both contestation and accommodation. "Instead of challenging state power directly, the Muslim Brotherhood and other reformist groups are involved in the gradual appropriation of the public space, creating new models of political leadership and community in contrast to the policies and practices of state elites. Though posing a moral alternative to the secular state, such groups are nevertheless dependent on patrons within it for support."[47] Lately, the government has been less tolerant toward the Ikhwan, utilizing both bureaucratic and coercive measures to curb their rising influence and popularity.

The regime's main priority of excluding Islamists from political participation by completely suppressing the militants and containing and harassing the moderates cannot be accomplished without sacrificing the few democratic steps adopted in the mid-to-late 1980s. What are the major developments of the 1990s which signify the retreat from democratization in Egypt?

The first blow to democratization has been the continuation of the emergency laws since 1981. In addition to the emergency laws, "terrorist laws" have been passed in parliament which make membership in a "terrorist organization," as defined by the state, a crime punishable by death, and ordains speedy trials by military courts for those arrested under these laws. The outcome of all this has been gross human rights violations by the state and increased violence by both the security forces and the militants.

Second, the intervention of the government in the affairs of independent syndicates in order to contain the rising popularity of moderate Islamists is a regression from democratic practice. A low point in this intervention is the syndicate law, which is likely to end the practice of honest elections within professional unions. Moderate Islamists and opposition leaders have described this law as a "stab in the back of democracy."[48] In the words of Fahmi Huwaidi, the new syndicate law "shocked us four times: once because it was issued, second because it was justified in the name of democracy; third because it was issued by the People's Assembly, and finally because some intellectuals and politicians welcomed it."[49] In addition, the government recently eliminated the right of professors to elect the deans of university faculties, and decreed that mayors and village council members will be appointed instead of elected. Many of those elected to these positions in recent years have been affiliated with the Ikhwan.

The third event in the retreat from democratization was the "re-election" of Mubarak for a third term and his reluctance to introduce political reform. "To many Egyptians, the referendum signals an end to hopes that Mubarak will institute real democratic reform," Chris Hedges of *The New York Times* reported on the eve of the referendum. He continued, "many say they believe that political renewal may come only at the point of a gun, as it has in the past."[50] Mubarak ran uncontested and was approved by 94.9 percent of the valid votes cast. Any hope that Mubarak would introduce change was shattered when he invited Atef Sidki, the same Prime Minister he has had since 1986, to form a government. No change was introduced to key ministries.[51]

A fourth illustration of the reversal of early democratization steps under Mubarak is the November-December 1995 elections. It was obvious even before the election that the government was working to deprive the opposition from gaining any significant representation and to assure an overwhelming majority for the ruling party (the National Democratic Party). The government concentrated its efforts on the largest and most popular opposition group, the Muslim Brotherhood. On November 23, less than a week before the election, a military court tried 82 leading members of the Ikhwan and sentenced 54 of them to jail terms of three or more years. Of those who were tried, 51 were candidates for the parliamentary elections.[52]

Election returns produced the result that the regime had in mind (see Table 5.5). The government "won," but the real loser was democracy. According to the independent Egyptian Human Rights Organization, which monitored the voting process, this was the worst election in Egypt's recent history. The Organization titled its December 28 report "The Elections Nobody Won" (*Intikhabat lam yanjah fiha ahad*). The report had nine main observations about the elections, including widespread violence in which at least forty were killed and hundreds injured in clashes between rival candidates; intimidation, harassment, and arrest of oppositional party candidates, and their expulsion from opposition stations; the stuffing of fake votes into the ballot boxes; and the refusal of the government to carry out court injunctions in cases of violations reported by candidates. The number of Ikhwan members arrested reached over one thousand. The report recommended that the resulting parliament be dissolved and called for a new election under the supervision of the judiciary and a neutral government.[53]

TABLE 5.5 The Results of the 1995 People's Assembly Election

Party	*Seats*	*Percent of Votes*
National Democratic	416	93.6
New Wafd	6	1.3
National Progressive Unionist	5	1.1
Liberal	1	0.2
Nasserite Arab Democratic	1	0.2
Independents*	15	3.3
Total	444	100

Note: *One of these independents is affiliated with the Ikhwan.
Sources: *Al-Hayat,* Dec. 8, 1995, p. 1; *Keesing's Record of World Events,* Vol. 42, no. 12, January 1996, p. 40879.

Finally, the regime's increasing pressure against the moderate Islamists, particularly Ikhwan, is expected to have grave consequences. In addition to the frequent harassment and arrests of local leaders of the movement and the attempt to weaken their influence in syndicates, unions, and local councils, government officials have been attempting to redefine radicalism to include even moderate reformists. Government figures refer to the Ikhwan as the other face of terrorism. The blurring of the distinction between moderate Ikhwan and militant Islamists will only widen the circle of repression, encourage more radicalization among Islamists, and increase the potential for violence. The spokesman for the Ikhwan, Ma'mun al-Hudaibi, was quoted as saying, "If our supporters believe we cannot achieve our goals peacefully, they may turn to more radical means to achieve them."[54]

Amid the increased violence and counterviolence, the government has manipulated secularist intellectuals in its war against Islamists by encouraging them to libel Islamists personally and to ridicule the "Islamic alternative" rather than offer substantive criticism of it. The recruitment of secularists, particularly communists, in the media war against Islamists is common to Egypt, Tunisia, and Algeria. The annual tradition of inviting leading intellectuals to debate public issues at the Cairo Book Fair, for example, has degenerated into a one-sided diatribe excoriating Islamists, whose participation in the event has been restricted recently. "The intellectual monologue 'against terrorism' at the Cairo Book Fair in January only proved how far secular intellectuals of the right and left are ready to play into the hands of the government."[55]

For some secularists, the lesser of the two evils—these being the regime and the Islamists—is the regime. As secular novelist Gamal al-Ghitani puts it, "In the battle between a religious extremism and terrorism seeking to bring down a corrupt and basically repressive Government, the choice for many of us, lamentable though it might be, is to side with army and regime."[56] There are "fundamentalist" secularists who totally reject any political role for Islamist movements, including the moderate Ikhwan. One example is Hussein Ahmed Amin, former ambassador and prolific author. In his opinion, any Islamist group will use democracy to gain power and then abolish the democratic process in favor of antidemocratic religious rule. He compares Islamists to Adolf Hitler. "If they do reach power, it would be too late. If we put them to the test and allow them to reach power, they will never share it. This applies to the Muslim Brotherhood as much as any other Islamic group or faction."[57]

To some Islamists, particularly the militants, the proclamations of these extremist secularists are not purely intellectual discourse, but rather a call for the exclusion from participation and a justification for the brutal, violent campaign by the security forces to eradicate Islamists. To militant Islamists, such individuals become a part of the oppressive state apparatus and deserve to be treated as such. It was under these circumstances that Farag Foda, the most outspoken anti-Islamist, was assassinated by militants in 1992. Foda was given a great deal of exposure and license by the official media to attack Islamists in general and to slander and libel Islamist individuals. While the Ikhwan were not fond of Foda, they joined opposition parties in condemning the assassination and the spread of violence.[58]

Although violent attempts against secular intellectuals has been limited, it could worsen if the vicious cycle continues and polarization between Islamists and secularists hardens further. Algeria is a lesson in point. There, extremist Islamists targeted secularists while secularists formed their own militias, joining government forces to eradicate Islamists through violence.[59]

The government strategy of recruiting secularists in its ideological campaign against the Islamists, coupled with attempts at excluding the moderate Ikhwan and equating them with the militants, increases polarization and could lead the country toward Algeria's unfortunate experience of civil war.

Finally, there is sporadic sectarian strife between Muslims and Copts in the southern part of the country, a stronghold of the militants and a place of relatively high concentrations of the Christian Coptic minority. The Copts already feel apprehensive at the prospect of an Islamist takeover, their fears exacerbated by violent clashes between members of their community and the militant Islamists. The government has used these sectarian clashes to justify the prolonging of martial law and the denial of legal status to any political party based on religion. Since no

Coptic group so far has attempted to form a political party, this policy is aimed at Islamists.

Limits and Prospects

Egypt has a head start over many other Arab nations in some of the factors which create favorable conditions for democracy. Collective identity, at least in the sense of agreement on borders and a sense of local cohesion, is relatively stable in Egypt. Nominal opposition and some limited freedom of expression could become a basis for political pluralism. The strongest opposition, the Ikhwan, is moderate and willing to work within the system if allowed. On the other hand, several factors militate against democracy in Egypt. Low resources, high population growth, and poor distribution of wealth widen the gap between haves and have-nots and create adverse economic conditions for democratization. Bureaucratic corruption in the government sabotages any attempt at reform. Mubarak's obtuse leadership botches opportunities and stubbornly disregards the rising cost of repression. The influence of world powers, notably the US, has a deleterious effect on democratization in Egypt, supporting an authoritarian status quo rather than risking change. All these contribute to Egypt's politics of exclusion and obstruct the path of democratization.

In the Arab world, postcolonial Egypt was not an artificial entity. Despite the various rules before and since the Arabo-Islamic conquest, its boundaries have not shifted very much. The late Egyptian historian Gamal Hamdan describes the characteristics which made Egypt unique and a center for other Arab countries: historical continuity, homogenous population, and a uniform agricultural region, in which the people have settled along the two banks of the Nile River.[60] Egypt's population is highly homogenous. The 1986 census showed that 94% of the people are Muslim (almost all Sunnis); the only substantial minority, at 5.8%, is the Copts, who in any case consider themselves the original inhabitants of the land of Egypt. Even as a minority, then, the Copts share with the majority a strong sense of Egyptianness. There are also about 50,000 Egyptian adherents of other Christian sects and a very small Jewish community.[61] The vast majority of the population, then, identifies as Egyptian, speaks Arabic (with a distinctive Egyptian dialect) and is Muslim by religion.

While there is a strong sense of Egyptian national identity among the population, there have been differences over what constitutes Egyptianness. As detailed in Chapter Two, local nationalism (*wataniyya*) in modern Egypt has its roots in Muhammad Ali's assertion of independence from Ottoman rule just after Napoleon's retreat from his Egyptian adventure. *Wataniyya* was strong during the British occupation, when the emphasis was on liberation from colonial rule. Nominal independence for Egypt came in 1923. The aristocratic and bourgeois nationalists who formed the ruling elite left in place by the British were totally discredited by the Arab failure to prevent Israeli occupation of Palestinian land in the 1948 war. Then came Nasser, who located Egyptian nationalism within the wider sphere of Arab nationalism and defined the role of Egypt as the natural leader of the Arab world. Under Sadat, Arabism was downplayed and Egyptianism was emphasized, with a touch of Islamic character. By the late 1980s, the Islamic identity of Egypt became even more central, reflected in the 1987 parliamentary election in which almost all political forces advocated the implementation of *shari`a* to varying degrees. Yet with the rise of radical Islamist groups, a countercoalition defending secularism (the separation of religion from politics) arose. This coalition is composed of small but influential leftist intellectuals, some members of the ruling elite, and many in the Coptic community. Nevertheless, the social homogeneity of Egypt and the strong sense of national unity are favorable conditions for the prospect of transition toward democracy.

Another positive factor for a movement toward democracy is the fact that Egypt's main Islamic movement, the Ikhwan, has been willing to work from within the system and has adhered to the rules of the democratic game. The Ikhwan has condemned violence as a matter of principle, whether committed by the government or by the militants.[62] To the Ikhwan, as one of their leaders states, much of the violence stems from the lack of genuine political participation and the repression by a corrupt government. "The young men who are involved in such radical activities could have been contained and tamed through a genuine democratic process in which their grievances would have found the way to settlement and resolution, and as a result violence would gradually fade out and eventually disappear."[63] Ikhwan leaders call *hiwar* (dialogue) "the forgotten obligation."[64] This is in contrast to the militants, who say that "the forgotten obligation" is armed struggle against the "ignorant and unIslamic regime."

Despite the democratic regression in Egypt, oppositional parties continue to function within the small margin of freedom allowed. More importantly, the press, including organs of the opposition, continues to enjoy a significant degree of freedom of expression, by the standards of the Arab world. The opposition has used this margin for freedom of expression to criticize the government, expose corruption, call for reform, and present itself as an alternative to Mubarak and his party. Major opposition parties, the Labor and Wafd in addition to the Ikhwan, have used the print media to adamantly oppose the renewal of Mubarak for a third term.[65] Although the government responded by arresting the deputychair of the Labor Party and two other journalists in the party's paper, *al-Sha`b*, they were released on October 7, 1993 under popular pressure. This incident highlights the classic dilemma of authoritarian regimes when they allow *glasnost*-like measures: how to contain the forces they unleash.

However, in spite of the existence of a strong sense of collective identity, a nominal opposition, a relatively free press, and a moderate Islamic movement committed to working from within the system, other factors are required for democracy to come about in Egypt. First, there must be substantial socioeconomic and political reform, in order for the root sources of corruption and violence to dry up. Although the International Monetary Fund and the World Bank provide Egypt with significant debt relief because of its stand on the Gulf War and give Egypt good grades on its structural reforms, these reforms have not improved the living conditions of most Egyptians. Unemployment, underemployment, lack of basic services, and poverty—all these have remained endemic.

The main economic challenge for Egypt is the growing gap between sustained population growth and natural resource depletion. For instance, Egypt's population today, an estimated 59 million, is expected to reach 65 million by the end of this decade. Simultaneously, according to one source, ten percent of Egypt's agriculture production is lost every year due to the deterioration of soil fertility.[66] It is logical to assume that Egypt's economic problems, regardless of its political system, can only be solved with regional cooperation and integration in which a portion of Egypt's labor force could get jobs in the underpopulated countries, especially neighboring Libya and the Arab Gulf states. What makes the matter worse is the extent of corruption and mismanagement within the government and the top bureaucracy. "Deals on every conceivable commodity are made by middlemen and commission agents, usually with some minister or Mubarak-in-law as a front."[67] Egypt has a tiny wealthy strata composed of the current and former officials (including many with military backgrounds) and private business tycoons who quietly enriched themselves during the early years of *infitah*, in contrast to the majority who are considered middle and lower class, but border on poverty. It is the first group that continues to benefit from the Mubarak regime and to support it in return. "To raise morale, and morality," Ahmed Abdallah suggests, "mount a serious campaign against corruption. Some present cabinet ministers are obvious candidates to stand trial." He adds, "Cleaning up the ruling party can pave the way for a coalition government, including moderate Islamists. This would set the course for expanding employment opportunities for the young,"[68] underscoring that a purge of corruption would help redress both economic and political hindrances to democracy.

Another extremely basic requirement for the move toward democracy is an end to the monopolization of power and the inclusion of the opposition in the political process. Abdallah suggests this as the crux of a "massive reform program:"

> At the political level this means ending the monopoly of power, changing the constitution, having elections for president and not just yes-or-no referenda. . . . Conduct local elections, leave the unions and professional associations alone, and, most importantly, incorporate the bulk of Islamists into the system by legalizing a non-violent Islamist party (the Muslim Brotherhood is the obvious choice.)[69]

The Ikhwan, as the largest and most popular opposition movement, constitutes a meaningful avenue to political participation for a large portion of marginalized Egyptians. The inclusion of the Ikhwan is absolutely necessary if political pluralism is to be credible. The reality is that the Mubarak regime, with the blessing of some secular forces, has opted for further exclusion and even repression. Mubarak has recently associated the Ikhwan with the militants and compared them with the zealots in Algeria, pledging that the Ikhwan would remain outlawed. "They are an illegal group who stand behind most of the religiously motivated acts of sabotage,"[70] Mubarak has said. The regime recently excluded them from the long-awaited conference on national dialogue, which took place June-July 1994. In protest, some of the other opposition groups refused to attend because of what they saw as an attempt by the government to "defuse opposition and isolate the mainstream Islamist political movement rather than as a means of seriously considering the need for political change."[71]

A third requirement for democratization is for those Western governments which have leverage over Egypt, particularly the US, to pressure Mubarak's regime to move toward democracy, or at least to improve its human rights records. The reality, however, is the West is concerned more about the stabilizing role of Egypt and its role in moderating other Arab regimes like that of Asad. Moreover, the fact that Islamists have become the viable alternative to Mubarak has complicated things for the Western powers, which are no less alarmed by the rise of Islamists than is the Mubarak regime. Even American journalists have noticed the reluctance of external powers to encourage democracy in Egypt. Citing the fact that Egypt has been the largest recipient of US foreign aid, after Israel, Hedges, Kaplan, and others note how little the US pushes the issue of democracy in Egypt. "While Egypt's basic services have significantly improved" as a result of US aid, "Washington has done little to alter the one-party state or dampen dissent."[72]

A successful transition to democracy would have the best chances under skilled leadership and competent political engineering. The reality is that Mubarak is a very inferior leader. He lacks the charisma of Nasser and Sadat's risk-taking initiative. Mubarak's staff members are mostly sycophantic military cronies and officials from previous regimes. According to Tahsin Bashir, former spokesperson for Sadat, Mubarak "looks around him and sees people who support him 110%. He no longer acknowledges the problems in Egypt and when he does acknowledge them, he blames them on conspiracies launched by his enemies. The objective reality that is pushing young people to rebel is beyond his grasp."[73] He is reported to have criticized Gorbachev and former Algerian President Benjedid for precipitating their own ousters by unleashing reform. The alternative for which Mubarak has opted is merely to preserve a cumbersome, inefficient, and corrupt system. As Muhammad Hassanein Heikal, prominent Egyptian journalist, sums up, the Mubarak government "has no ideas, no vision, no values."[74] The overwhelming economic problems of Egypt, Western support for the status quo and the international community's failure to pressure the regime to democratize, the regime's determination to exclude the Ikhwan from the political process, and the lack of competent leadership makes the prospects for democracy in Egypt bleak.

In June 1991, nine opposition parties joined the unrecognized Ikhwan to demand political reform. The Ikhwan and the nine parties (Wafd, Labor, Liberal, NPUP, Nation, Young Egypt, Green, Democratic Unionist, and Social Arab) reached a consensus on the basis of this reform which they formulated in a ten-point statement calling for:

1. Commitment to the human rights and public liberties mentioned in *shari`a* and international law;
2. An end to the state of emergency and martial law;
3. A lift of restrictions on the formation of political parties;
4. The independent supervision of elections by the judiciary;
5. The adoption of the parliamentary system in which the executive power will be vested in the Cabinet, which is selected from the party with the majority;
6. Guarantee of the right of the People's Assembly to amend the budget; granting the Shura Council powers of oversight and legislation;
7. Choice of the president through direct election from a list of several candidates, with a limit of two terms;
8. The compatibility of all legislation passed with *shari`a,* with emphasis on the rights of non-Muslims to follow their own religious law in case of contradiction;
9. The independence of the judiciary;

10. Liberation of the press and media from government control and equal opportunity for all political parties in the official media.[75]

These demands for democratic practices are comprehensive and far-reaching. In order to implement some of these demands, the constitution would have to be amended.

The Mubarak government's response varied from strong condemnation of the opposition to ridicule of its leading figures.[76] The regime's refusal to concede to the demands of the opposition has not improved political conditions. On the contrary, political violence has intensified, human rights violations have increased, and radicalization and polarization have risen. The Egyptian regime has not exhausted the repression option. However, the violence will only breed more violence, as the events of the last two years have proved. Mubarak believes that the lesson of Algeria is "do not democratize because that will mean granting power to Islamists." Perhaps a better lesson to be learned from Algeria is that if the state begins to democratize, and then reneges on democratization promises and uses its military and security apparatus to suppress brutally such a popular oppositional force as Islamists, no one will be able to control the cycle of violence that will ensue.

Notes

1. Many intellectuals, especially secularists and leftists, blamed Sadat for the rise of radical Islamic groups because he seemed to tolerate and encourage their activities as a counter-force against Nasserites and other leftists.

2. "Egypt," *The Middle East and North Africa 1993*, 39th ed. (London: Europa Publications Ltd., 1992), p. 368.

3. For the negative consequences of the economic opening see Gouda Abdel Khalek, "The Open Door Economic Policy in Egypt: Its Contribution to Investment and Its Equity Implications," in Malcolm Kerr and El-Sayed Yassin, eds., *Rich and Poor States in the Middle East: Egypt and the New Arab Order* (Boulder, CO: Westview Press, 1982), pp. 259–83.

4. See, for example, "The Road to Peace," in Sadat's autobiography *In Search of Identity* (New York, NY: Harper & Row, 1978) pp. 271–313.

5. Sadat's irritation with the Soviets is amply detailed in Chapters Eight and Nine of his autobiography. Ibid., pp. 204–231. He believed that ninety-nine percent of the solution to the Arab-Israeli conflict lay in the hands of the U.S.

6. For example, he was involved in an attempt to create a federation with Libya, Sudan, and Syria, which eventually failed.

7. "Egypt," p. 309.

8. This is the function of "parliaments" in most Arab states.

9. EIU Country Profile 1994/95, *Egypt* (London: the Economist Intelligence Unit, 1994), p. 5.

10. For an account of the crackdown on opposition and subsequent developments, see Mohamed Heikal, *Autumn of Fury: The Assassination of Sadat* (New York, NY: Random House, 1983).

11. Main sources of this survey are: EIU Country Profile 1994/95, *Egypt*; and "Egypt" in *The Middle East and North Africa*, p. 369–376.

12. "Egypt," p. 370.

13. In a personal interview with Ma'mun al-Hudaibi, official Ikhwan spokesman who contested and won a seat in this election, he gave me numerous examples of government harassment against opposition candidates. In his case, these measures included the arrest of some of his relatives on election day to occupy him from following the election procedures and ensuring their fairness. Cairo, Aug. 11, 1993.

14. "Egypt," p. 374. In a personal interview with a former police officer (requesting anonymity) who had been in charge of one polling center in 1989, he told me that two hours before the polls at his center were due to close, he listened in amazement as a voice on the radio broadcast the election results from his center. Cairo, Aug. 13 1993.

15. Mahmud Akef and Muhammad Ghurab, *al-Umma fi Am: Taqrir Hawli An al-Shu'oon al-Siyasiyya wal Iqtisadiyya al-Masriyya 1990–1991* (The Nation in a Year: An Annual Report on Egyptian Political and Economic Affairs 1990–1991) (Cairo: Umma Press & al-Istishariyyun al-`Arab, 1991), p. 205.

16. "Li Awal Mara: Tasjil Sawti li Zaki Badr Yuthbit Kulla Baza'atihi" (For the first time: An audio recording of Zaki Badr's voice proves all his profanity), *al-Sha`b*, January 9, 199, p. 1.

17. For a detailed account of the parties' positions toward the elections see Akef and Ghurab, eds., *al-Umma Fi Am*, pp. 99–207.

18. EIU Country Profile, *Egypt*, p. 5.

19. Reported in Akef and Ghurab, *al-Umma Fi Am*, pp. 127–128.

20. In a personal interview with leading Ikhwan figure and former member of Parliament Muhammad Faiz Akef, he mentioned that even the leftist NPUP had formed a bureau for shari'a. Cairo, Aug. 14, 1993.

21. For a listing of the amendments, see "Egypt," pp. 395–396.

22. *Ma'alim fil Tariq* (Milestones) (Cairo: Dar al- Shuruq, 1980).

23. See, for instance, Rafa`t Said Ahmed, *Tanzimat al-Ghadab al-Islami fi al-Sab`inat* (The Organizations of Islamic Rage in the Seventies) (Cairo: Maktabat Madbuli, 1989), p. 126.

24. Ibid., pp. 42–43.

25. Personal interview, Cairo, Aug. 13, 1993.

26. The Ikhwan were allowed twice to publish their own magazine. First they published *al-Da`wa* in the late 1970s which later was closed when Sadat cracked down on the opposition in 1981, and in the late 1980s they took over the management of a private magazine, *Liwa' al-Islam*, which was eventually forced to shut down because of its criticism of the government during the Gulf War. Recently, the Ikhwan has resumed publication of *al-Da`wa* from London.

27. Essam Al-Erian, "The Future of Power-Sharing in Egypt," in Azzam Tamimi, ed., *Power-Sharing Islam?* (London: Liberty for Muslim World Publications, 1993), p. 168.

28. The speeches of the Ikhwan figures to Parliament between 1987 and 1988 are collected in Mohsen Radi, ed., *al-Ikhwan Tahta Qubat al- Barlaman* (The Ikhwan Under the Parliamentary Rotunda) (Cairo: Dar al-Tawzi' wal Nashr al-Islamiyya, 1990).

29. *Al-Mujtama` al-Madani* (Civil Society), No. 23, Nov. 1993, p. 7.

30. "Lawyers' Fury," *Civil Society*, Vol. 3, Issue 30, June 1994, p. 4.

31. *Al-Ahram*, Aug. 15, 1993, p. 1.

32. For a summary of the government's security measures, see the EIU, *Egypt*, p. 11.

33. This figure is current up to December 3, 1994. *New York Times*, December 4, 1994, p. 6.

34. Whenever clashes take place between security forces and militant Islamists, the government claims to have captured "the most dangerous cell of the terrorists" or "the fugitive leader," etc. For one example, see "Mulahaqat al-Mutatarifin fi Misr" (The Hunt for Extremists in Egypt), *al-Majala*, Dec. 25, 1992, p. 24.

35. On splits within the militant groups see "Khilafat wa Inshiqaqat Muthira Ta`sif bi al-Jihad" (Inflammatory disagreements and splits storm through al-Jihad), *al-Wasat*, No. 83, Aug. 30, 1993, p. 35.

36. See the EIU Country Report 3rd quarter 1994, *Egypt* (London: The Economist Intelligence Unit, 1994).

37. In my interviews with them, the Ikhwan leaders were very critical of the government's implementation of emergency laws and of the security forces' systematic efforts to harass them.

38. Al-Erian, "The Future . . . ," p. 163.

39. "Eaten from Within," *Atlantic Monthly*, Nov. 1994, p. 28.

40. Chris Hedges, "Egypt Begins Crackdown on Strongest Opposition Group," *New York Times*, June 12, 1994.

41. Al-Erian, "The Future . . . ," p. 166. The figure about the philanthropies is mentioned by Hedges, ibid.

42. Government control of mosques in many cases means that the government pays for the salary of the imam and for the physical maintenance of the mosque. The extent of ideological control over sermons and administration varies from case to case.

43. "Al-Muhafaza wal Taqadum fi Misr: Al-Ihya' al-Islami" (Conservatism and Progressivism in Egypt: The Islamic Revival), *Qira'at Siyasiyya*, Vol. 3, No. 2, Spring 1993, p. 19.

44. Ibid., p. 19.

45. For a summary of the Salsabil affair, see Mahmud Akef ed., *al-Umma fi Amm 1991–1992* (The Nation in a Year 1991–1992) (Cairo: Markaz al-Dirasat al-Hadhariyya, 1992), p. 286.

46. EIU Country Profile, *Egypt*, p. 6.

47. Carrie Rosefsky Wickham, "Beyond Democratization: Political Change in the Arab World," *PS Political Science and Politics*, Vol. 27, No. 3, Sept. 1994, p. 508.

48. Al-Erian, "The Future . . . ," p. 166.

49. "Ijhad al-Hulm al-Dimoqrati fi Misr," (The Abortion of the Democratic Dream in Egypt), *Qira'at Siyasiyya*, Vol. 7, No. 2, Spring 1993, p. 139.

50. "As Egypt Votes on Mubarak, He Faces Rising Peril," Oct. 4, 1993, p. A8.

51. *Keesing's Record of World Events*, Vol. 39, No. 10, 1993, p. 39711.

52. "The Higher Military Court Passes Its Ruling in the Case of the Muslim Brotherhood," *al-Wafd*, Nov. 24, 1995, pp. 1 and 8.

53. "The Final Report of the Egyptian Human Rights Organization," *al-Wafd*, Dec. 29, 1995, pp. 1 and 3.

54. Chris Hedges, "Egypt Begins Crackdown on Strongest Opposition Groups," *New York Times*, June 12, 1994, p. 5.

55. Ahmed Abdallah, "Egypt's Islamists and the State: From Complicity to Confrontation," *Middle East Report*, July-Aug. 1993, p. 30.

56. Edward Said, "The Phony Islamic Threat," *New York Times Magazine*, November 21, 1993, p. 64.

57. "Interview with Hussein Ahmed Amin," *Civil Society*, Vol. 3, Issue 33, Sept. 1994, p. 27.

58. *Al-Sha'b*, June 16, 1992, p. 2.

59. Arabic newspapers such as *al-Hayat* use the term "eradicators" to describe the junta and secularists in Algeria because they advocate the total extermination of Islamists, as opposed to dialogue.

60. *Shakhsiyyat Misr: Dirasa fi Abqariyat al-Makan* (Egypt's Personality: A Study of the Genius of the Place) (Cairo: Maktabat al-Nahda al-Misriyya, 1970), p. 7.

61. EIU Country Profile, *Egypt*, p. 11.

62. *Bayan min al-Ikhwan al-Muslimin Hawla Mawjat al-Unf wal Irhab* (Communique from the Ikhwan about the Wave of Violence and Terrorism), Mar. 3, 1993.

63. Al-Erian, "The Future . . . ," p. 167.

64. See the section on al-hiwar (dialogue) in Akef, *al-Umma Fi Am*, p. 301.

65. See the editorial in *al-Wafd*, "al-Shu`ub al-Hurra la Tuaqi` Ala Bayad" (Free Peoples Do Not Sign Blank Checks), Aug. 12, 1993, p. 1; and the Labor party publication by Hilmi Murad and Adel Hussein, *Limaza Naqul La Fi Istitla` al-Ri'asa al-Qadima* (Why we say no to the coming presidential referendum).

66. Kaplan, "Eaten From Within," p. 42.

67. Said, "The Phony Islamic Threat," p. 64. For an insider view of corruption in the government see Tahsin Bashir,"Risalla Maftuha Ila al-Ra'is Mubarak" (An Open Letter to President Mubarak), *al-Wafd* , Sept. 3, 1992, p. 5.

68. "Egypt's Islamists and the State," p. 30.

69. Ibid., p. 30.

70. EIU Country Report 3rd quarter 1994, *Egypt*, p. 10.

71. Ibid., p. 10–11.

72. Hedges, "As Egypt Votes on Mubarak, He Faces Rising Peril," *New York Times*, Oct. 4, 1993, p. A8.

73. Ibid, p. A8.

74. Said, "The Phony Islamic Threat," p. 63. See too the evaluation of Mubarak's regime by eleven prominent figures from his party and the opposition in Muhammad al-Tawil, *Kaifa Yusna` al-Qarar fi Misr* (How Decisions Are Made in Egypt) (Cairo: Star, 1992).

75. The ten points are listed in El-Sayed Yassin ed., *al-Taqrir al-Istratiji al-Arabi 1991* (The Arab Strategic Report 1991) (Cairo: Markaz al-Dirasat al-Istratijiyya fil Ahram, 1992), p. 385.

76. See, for example, "Khitab al-Ra'is Mubarak bi Munasabat Thawrat Yulio" (President Mubarak's Speech on the Anniversary of the July Revolution), *al-Gumhuriyya*, July 23, 1991, p. 1.

6

Jordan: A Case of Inclusion

By 1993, Jordan had emerged as the most democratically open country in the Arab world. Broadly speaking, the level of genuine political participation available to average Jordanians is greater than that available to most other Arab peoples. Inhabitants of Jordan expect and enjoy, among other things, a wider margin of freedom of the press, of speech, and of assembly than the margins generally allowed in other Arab countries, to varying but significant degrees. How has this state of things developed in Jordan? To what degree is Jordan a case of successful democratization? What are the limits and flaws of Jordanian democratization as it unfolds today?

Jordan's King Hussein made a decision to go ahead with the second parliamentary election in November 1993,[1] despite the risks it posed to the regional peace negotiations and to his role in them (not least of which was the risk posed by allowing definitions of Jordanian and Palestinian collective identity to be contested in the public arena at that moment). In this way, the momentum from the democratization initiatives of 1989 was not lost. Continuity in the democratization process was maintained—with one significant change: The regime altered the electoral law, as will be detailed below, to reduce the power of oppositional forces. After a protest against the changes in electoral law, almost all parties participated in the election. As anticipated by the government, the election produced a proregime assembly.

The affair of the electoral law alterations demonstrates the limits of Jordan's democratic experiment. Nevertheless, unlike other Arab countries, Jordan has not reversed course from its early democratization. Jordan belongs at the top of any chart measuring the relative democratic openness of Arab states. What constitutes Jordan's democratic openness since 1989? How has the struggle of the Jordanian polity to articulate a collective identity worked itself out in the qualified success of the country's democratic experiment? How do regional and local conditions provide a context for this experiment? It is worthwhile first to understand the history from which Jordan's contemporary democratic experiences emerge.

Historical Background

The history of Jordan as an independent state is a relatively short one. It began in 1921 when the League of Nations gave Britain "mandate" power over lands which it then divided into Palestine and Transjordan. Britain recognized Abdullah as a prince of central authority over Transjordan. In March 1946, Transjordan became independent. Shortly thereafter, Abdullah assumed the title of king. Transjordan took part in the first Arab-Israeli war in 1948, which left Transjordan with control of a Palestinian territory, the West Bank (including East Jerusalem), and with a large number of Palestinian refugees forced out of their homes by the Zionist state. This development would have enormous repercussions on the development of the Jordanian state for years to come. Subsequently, King Abdullah annexed the West Bank in April 1950 and unified it with Transjordan to form the Hashemite Kingdom of Jordan. Abdullah ruled until his assassination in 1951; he was succeeded by his son Talal, who was quickly removed from office on the grounds of poor mental health. In 1952, Talal's 17 year old son Hussein was proclaimed king. The history of Jordan since then has occurred under the tenure of Hussein, the longest reigning head-of-state in the region.

The first major political development in the state of Jordan was the adoption of a new constitution in 1952, a few months before Hussein's inauguration. Jordan was proclaimed a constitutional monarchy, with authority jointly exercised by the king and a National Assembly. The Constitution, still in effect today, is considered liberal because it establishes citizens' basic rights and freedoms and makes the cabinet partially accountable to the National Assembly. However, the Constitution also vests extensive executive powers in the hands of the king. He is the commander of the armed forces; appoints the prime minister and the cabinet; convenes and dissolves the Assembly; and orders general elections. Although the Assembly, in theory, has the right to override the king's veto of legislation, the King has been able to maintain superiority over the Assembly, often by dissolving it whenever it challenges him.[2]

The period from 1953 to 1974 was marked by a series of crises for the King, starting with a challenge at home by nationalist-leftist forces motivated by Gamal Abdul Nasser. It was during this confrontation that Jordan's first democratic interlude occurred. In October 1956, Jordan had its first free, multiparty parliamentary election. The issues: the end of Jordan's treaty with Britain; rapprochement with Egypt; and calls for more freedoms for the people and the press. The results approximate the dominant mood of many Arab countries during the period: Of forty contested seats, the Socialist National Party got eleven; the Muslim Brotherhood, four; the Constitutional Party, three; the Communist Party, three; the

Ba`th, two, and the Liberation Party, one. The Socialist Nationalists won on a platform of Arab unity, opposition to British influence, and rejection of the Baghdad Pact (an anti-Nasser agreement between Britain, Iraq, Turkey, and Iran).

Because the Socialist National Party got most of these votes, the King asked its leader, Suleiman al-Nabulsi, to form the new government despite his failure to win a seat in parliament. The new government tried to implement a nationalist agenda, including the abrogation of the treaty with Britain and the development of agreements with Syria, Egypt, and Saudi Arabia to replace British financial aid by forming an Arab solidarity front. Domestically, the government allowed a free hand to political parties and improved the freedom of the press. It became increasingly obvious to the King that the new government was trying to strip him of his authority gradually and to exercise executive power. Moreover, the nationalist and socialist orientation of the government conflicted with the King's moderate and conservative approach to foreign policy. For these reasons, the King saw the nationalist and leftist forces as undermining the very basis of the Kingdom in concert with outside forces (Nasser and the Soviets).[3]

The King asked al-Nabulsi to resign five months after the formation of his government. Al-Nabulsi's replacement by a prime minister loyal to the King did not go unnoticed. Demonstrations and protest led the loyalist government to declare martial law, dissolve political parties, and adjourn the extraordinary session of parliament; parliament itself was eventually dissolved altogether in 1961. The Nationalists' willingness to bypass the King and challenge the Constitution, as well as external pressure from nationalist Arab regimes (Syria and Egypt) on one side and world powers (Britain and the US) on the other precipitated the failure of this early democratic episode in Jordan.[4]

The second serious challenge to the King was the loss of the West Bank and its beloved East Jerusalem to Israel in 1967. King Hussein, like the leaders of Egypt and Syria, survived this blow, but it led to the influx of more Palestinian refugees and consequently to some destabilization in the Kingdom. From 1968 to 1971 Jordan witnessed the most serious internal strife in its history. The various Palestinian *feda'iyeen* (commandos) formed a state-within-a-state and launched attacks against the Israeli Occupation from Jordanian territory. This Palestinian challenge to Jordanian authority led to a face-off: A short but bloody war broke out between Palestinian guerrillas and loyalist Jordanian armed forces. Syrian intervention in favor of the Palestinians was deterred by Israel, which was eager to help Jordan quell the Palestinians. The Jordanians won, and the Palestinian *feda'iyeen* were expelled to Lebanon in 1971. On the other hand, Hussein's 1974 acceptance of the Rabat Arab summit decision recognizing the PLO as the sole legitimate representative of the Palestinians was a milestone in the conflict over who represented the Palestinians.

Although the regime and the country weathered this conflict, as it had the war of 1967 and the nationalist challenge of the 1950s, these crises had a destructive effect on the democratic process. They provided Hussein with justification for dissolving parliament and monopolizing political power. As Gubser notes, "parliamentary elections were either rigidly regulated or, if a measure of freedom of choice was allowed, the parliament was soon brought under control—for example, by changing members—or it was simply dismissed."[5]

It is important to note, however, that the Jordanian regime, unlike most of the other monarchies in the Arab world, has always felt the imperative to have some sort of consultative body, no matter how ineffectual this body may have been at times. During the 1970s the government created the Jordanian National Union in an attempt to fill the political vacuum left by the 1971 Civil War. This entity, intended as an alternative to political parties, failed miserably and was dissolved after two years.

The King had maintained martial law since 1967. Except in 1976, parliament had not met since 1974 (and would not meet until 1984). In 1978 the King addressed this gap by again seeking an alternative to parliament; he created a quasiparliament, the Consultative National Council. This Council was supposed to carry on some of the functions of parliament. Oddly enough, its sixty members ended up being very representative of the various political forces and the regional and demographic make-up of Jordan, despite being appointed and not elected.[6] In 1984, the King dissolved the third Council and recalled the previous parliament (National Assembly). Elections were then held to fill the eight seats of representatives who had died in the interim since parliament had last met. With these elections, the gears of democratization began to turn once more.

The period from 1971 to 1984 was for Jordan one of relative domestic stability and economic prosperity. It was also a period in which Jordan had no representative assembly. Prosperity brought improvements in standard of living, health, and education, raising the expectations Jordanians had of their government. At the same time, the lack of a parliament frustrated the people's ability to impose any accountability on their government when it failed to meet those expectations.

The Democratic Experiment Since 1989

The parliamentary election of November 1989 marked the beginning of new Jordanian democratization. That this election was not a token gesture was indicated by moves that accompanied and followed it: the reduction of the power of the extraordinary courts and the *mukhabarat* (secret service); the release of some political prisoners; the return of passports that had been confiscated to prevent regime opponents from traveling; the granting of more freedom to the press; the adoption of a National Charter in June 1991 (which became a Constitutional document in July 1992); and the end of martial law in the same year. Finally in 1992, parliament passed the Political Parties Act, allowing the legal formation of parties. Before the second parliamentary elections in November 1993, the government had licensed about twenty political parties covering a wide spectrum from right to left.

The 1989 elections were significant in many ways. They were the first general elections in twenty years. They were fair and free. They happened in a year of rapid worldwide change, about which the Jordanian people were as excited as anyone.[7] All political forces participated in the election. Although political parties were not yet legal at that point, prominent figures commonly known to be affiliated with various parties ran in the election. The results did not match what the King would have liked (see Table 6.1). In a thinly coded rebuke of Islamists, Hussein called for "objective and responsible dialogue within the framework of centrism, moderation, and rationality" and blasted "the exploitation of religion and the use of it as a means to achieve political objectives."[8] Islamists won anyway. Islamist victories and those of other oppositional figures gave credibility to the process, and proved that these elections constituted a significant move toward democracy for Jordan.

How do we account for the transformation in Jordan? How do we evaluate its success or lack of success? Four major forces come together to produce Jordan's experience with democracy: socioeconomic context; Jordanian resolution of the identity issue; the role of the Islamists; and the role of the king. Social and economic conditions in contemporary Jordan have yielded a society that is ready for the responsibilities of representative government and able to demand it. Simultaneously, Jordan has arrived at a point in its history at which debates over collective identity have subsided and something of an understanding over "who is Jordanian" and "what is Jordan" has congealed. Meanwhile, the major players in the tug-of-war for political power—in shorthand, the Islamists and the King—have accepted the boundaries and ground rules of the contest. The nature, characteristics, policies, and tactics of Islamists and King are important variables in the uniquely Jordanian democratic experience. How exactly these forces have composed that experience requires closer investigation.

Socioeconomic Context

By the 1980s, Jordanian society was highly urbanized, had developed one of the highest literacy rates in the Arab world,[9] and had a stable sense of

TABLE 6.1 1989 Jordanian Parliamentary Election Results

Affiliations	*Seats*	*Percent*
Muslim Brotherhood	22	27.5
Other Islamists	12	15.0
Nationalists	7	8.75
Leftists	4	5.0
Progovernment (former officials, traditionalists, community, and tribal leaders)	35	43.75
Total	80	100

Sources: Keesing's Record of World Events, Nov. 1989, p. 37052; *Middle East International,* Nov. 17, 1989, p. 3.

Jordanian identity shared by large portion of its inhabitants. These social and economic conditions, given the Jordanian regime's history of seeking legitimacy in some sort of consent from its people, produced among the average Jordanian expectations of democratic measures. The discrepancy between expectations and available options, as in many other cases of sociopolitical transformation, provided the impetus for change.

What immediately triggered the regime's adoption of the democratic measures in 1989 were the riots and disturbances which erupted in the southern part of the country that spring. Jordan had struggled with a domestic economic crisis in the mid-to-late 1980s on the heels of relative prosperity. The boom of the 1970s had created a large urban middle class and a high level of education, two conditions widely acknowledged as favorable for democratization. However, economic conditions began to deteriorate in the early 1980s. The problem lay in the decline in oil prices, which had two effects. First, it cut the employment rate for expatriate Jordanians in oil-producing countries, and second, it led these states to reduce their aid donations to Jordan. The impact of the economic deterioration was delayed until 1988–1989 because Jordan relied on commercial loans. It was near the end of the decade before a marked decline in Jordan's standard of living became apparent. For instance, per capita income fell from about $1,570 in 1985 to $980 in 1990, and unemployment hit an all-time peak of 30 percent early in the same year.[10] In addition, an authoritarian style of government had accompanied the economic crisis, along with nepotism, corruption, and harassment of people by the *mukhabarat* (secret police). The last straw for the populace was when the government, at the insistence of the International Monetary Fund, raised the price of basic commodities. As in Egypt in 1977 and Algeria in 1988, these measures provoked large-scale rioting. Protesters in a number of towns in southern Jordan demanded not only cancellation of the price hikes, but the resignation of the government of Zaid al-Rifa`i. Hussein was particularly alarmed by the protests because they came from his Jordanian (not Palestinian) subjects in the south, his major power base.

Jordan experienced great social transformation in the 1970s, changes with which its political development did not keep pace. Greater educational opportunities and relative economic prosperity raised people's level of expectations and capability without providing them with a commensurate voice in the decisions affecting their lives. Even the drafters of the National Charter acknowledged this discrepancy between the social and educational progress caused by the 1970s boom and, on the other hand, the stalled state of political participation. "Absence of popular participation and the monopoly on making economic and political decisions had a great role in the deterioration of public performance and the lack of trust between the citizens and the state," the drafters write.[11] Then came the protests in response to the economic policy, sending a clear message that the people wanted change. Not only did Hussein accept the demands of the rioters, he instructed the new prime minister to prepare for a return to parliamentary life, to uproot favoritism and corruption, and to end the politicization of religion.[12]

Jordanian Identity

One of the main assumptions of this study is that a sense of national identity is a prerequisite for the transition to democracy. While most Arab countries are still struggling to define who they are and what constitutes the crucial elements of their identity, they are generally resigned to their current "national" boundaries and attempt to define themselves within those boundaries. The real identity debate in most Arab countries today is about the centrality of Islam in defining the national community; it is a debate between advocates of "the Islamic solution" and those who reject any central role for Islam. What is the shape of Jordan nationalism today? How is the struggle over self-definition expressed in Jordanian politics?

When Britain created a central authority in Amman and crowned a prince from Arabia as its king, Jordan was perceived as one of the most artificial entities in the Arab world. It was not unusual for many to question whether such entity could survive and create a sense of nationhood about itself. Seventy-some years after its concoction, a center of loyalty has evolved, including masses of people who have invested a great deal in identifying themselves as "Jordanians."

Although King Hussein deserves much of the credit for the consolidation of Jordanian national identity, the moment of its birth was 1922, when Prince Abdullah was crowned head of Transjordan. His issuance of the first Jordanian National Charter in 1928 made this new identity official.[13] Being an newcomer to the area and lacking economic resources, Prince Abdullah realized from the beginning that his rule would have to be based, in significant degree, on consent. The inhabitants of Transjordan were a heterogenous mix of Bedouin tribes, the settled descendants of such tribes, and Circassian and Christian minorities. Abdullah's successful manipulation of tribal loyalties and Britain's economic and security support initially assured the survival of the new entity. After the war of 1948 and the incorporation of the West Bank into the Hashemite Kingdom, a new difficulty arose, that of integrating the Palestinian population into Jordan.

When young Hussein assumed the throne in 1952, he had to address two major threats to his rule: the challenge from nationalist and leftist forces and the impact of the Palestinian situation on his country. Hussein coped with these problems with a multifaceted strategy. First, he continued his grandfather's tradition of building a loyal constituency and deriving strength from it. He managed to enlarge this loyal base to include prominent families and heads of tribes, as well as Circassian and Palestinian notables. He did this by co-opting them into powerful positions and offering economic provisions from the state. Second, Hussein strengthened the institutions of the state, especially the army and the *mukhabarat* (secret police). What consolidated the army in Jordan, in contrast to other Arab countries, was its faithfulness to the head of state and its lack of politicization. Third, Hussein followed a moderate path in foreign policy, maintaining close relations with certain external powers which were interested in Jordan's survival, from Britain and the United States to the Arab Gulf states, Syria, Iraq, and even Israel. Jordan's strong ties with outside powers has been important as a source of income, income with which Hussein could pursue the first two strategies.

The monarchy's successful weathering of the troubled years in the 1950s, 1960s, and the Civil War years, strengthened Jordanian nationalism. The impact of the Civil War can not be overemphasized. The Palestinian *feda'iyeen* threatened the very existence of Jordan as a political entity. Royal army victory over the guerrillas not only removed that threat, but consolidated the identity of East Bankers as Jordanians. Simultaneously, the war emphasized the rise of an independent Palestinian identity both in the West Bank and in the Palestinian diaspora. In addition, the effect of the oil boom and the relative political stability of Jordan throughout the 1970s worked to the advantage of specific sectors, particularly those well-to-do Palestinians who had a stake in the survival of the Jordanian state.

Nevertheless, the Palestinian "question" continued to be a daunting one for Hussein, even after he recognized the PLO as the sole representative of the Palestinian people.[14] Not only are Palestinians 40–60% of Jordan's population, but the Arab-Israeli conflict is a continuing security threat for Jordan. For example, the claim made by some Israelis toward 1987 that "Jordan is Palestine" caused real alarm in Jordan. The notion that the Palestinian problem could be solved by overthrowing Hussein and establishing a Palestinian state in place of Jordan was pushed by Israeli hardliners such as Ariel Sharon.

However, events on the ground belied Israeli polemics and pointed to a distinct, if complex, Palestinian identity. The Intifadah in the Occupied Lands strengthened the Palestinian sense of nationalism and finally convinced Hussein that he did not represent the Palestinians. In 1988, Hussein decided to sever legal, fiscal, and administrative relations between the state of Jordan and the West Bank, a step welcomed by Jordanian nationalists on the East Bank. Consequently, Palestinians living in the West Bank were no longer considered Jordanian citizens, and they would not be represented in the parliament nor have the right to vote in elections. They were still allowed to carry Jordanian passports, but henceforth these would only have the status of 'travel documents.' However, Hussein stopped short of repealing the Union Agreement of 1950 in which Jordan had annexed the West Bank, thus leaving room open for future Jordanian involvement.[15]

When Hussein decided to restore parliament, then, he was using democratization as a defensive mechanism against the Israeli threat by pointing to the distinct and consensual nature of the Jordanian polity. In his opening speech immediately following the 1989 elections, Hussein stated that "parliament's return was a riposte to our enemies . . . who speculated that our country was on the verge of entering a dark labyrinth." Israel, he pointedly remarked, now had "to admit that the only solution to the Palestinian problem is recognizing Palestinian rights on Palestinian national soil."[16]

The question of Jordanian identity has not been contested by the religious and ethnic minorities which constitute around five percent of the population. The four percent of Jordan's population which is Christian (including Roman Catholic, Anglican, Coptic, and Greek Orthodox) enjoy generally amicable relations with their Muslim co-citizens and are guaranteed nine seats in parliament (11% of the total). The Circassians and Shishanis,[17] small Sunni Muslim ethnic minorities numbering 25,000 and 2,000 respectively, have a total of three seats in parliament but "occupy important positions in the armed forces and in other sensitive areas, and are acknowledged as being fiercely loyal to the throne."[18] As for the Palestinians, those who entered Jordan in 1948 are highly assimilated. Those who entered after 1967 and remain in refugee camps with very poor living conditions are disaffected with Jordan, while the most recent

Palestinian immigrants, who came back to Jordan as a result of the Gulf crisis and war, are wealthier and feel they have a stake in the Jordanian system.[19]

Whatever the outcome of the peace process, it is not likely to happen at Jordan's expense. Hussein has finagled from the peace agreements a prominent place for Jordan in the Middle East of the future, a place that seems secure even after his eventual exit from the political scene. The major part of Jordan's inhabitants today identify themselves as Jordanian and have a greater interest in the preservation of this political entity. Since this corresponds with the interests of both regional and world powers, the country Winston Churchill once boasted he created "on a Sunday afternoon" is here to stay.[20]

Islamists: The Reasonable Challengers[21]

Islamists have co-existed peacefully with the Jordanian regime and have proven to be a stabilizing factor in the country's political life. Jordan's experience with Islamic resurgence in recent years has been similar to that of other Arab countries. In the case of Jordan it is not difficult to gauge the power of Islamists, who came first in two parliamentary elections (1989 and 1993) and won elections within professional organizations and among university students. The King, on his side, has tolerated the Islamist movement for the most part, and has allowed it in recent years to participate in the democratic experiment. The inclusion of Islamists in the political process in Jordan is a successful model relative to other Arab countries. Cases of inclusion occur in Yemen, Kuwait, and Lebanon, but in most other Arab countries the regimes have enacted confrontational, repressive, and exclusionary policies toward Islamists. How can the reasonable working relationship between Islamists and the regime in Jordan be explained?

The term "Islamist movement" in Jordan refers mainly to the Ikhwan (the Muslim Brotherhood), which was never declared illegal. From its establishment in 1946, the Jordanian Ikhwan has been a legal organization; its operations have been public and open to scrutiny; it has worked within the Jordanian system. While this sounds normal, one must keep in mind that this precisely is not the norm in other Arab countries. Islamists were banned from establishing political parties in Egypt and Tunisia, for example. In Syria, the most extreme case, belonging to the Muslim Brotherhood is a crime punishable by death.

Now, the Ikhwan is not the only Islamist organization in Jordan. There are two other categories of Islamists. One is composed of independent Islamists who are close to the Ikhwan in objectives and method, but split from its ranks for one reason or another. These independents believe, like the Ikhwan, in working through the political system. They won twelve seats in the 1989 election. The second category is the Tahrir (Liberation) Party, formed in the mid-1950s in the West Bank, and at one point popular among Palestinians. This party has always been harshly critical of the monarchy, blaming King Hussein and his grandfather for the loss of Palestine, and regarding them both as puppets of Western powers. Members of this party have been suppressed by the *mukhabarat*. Tahrir's real lack of a wide base among the populace comes from the party's outdated discourse and extremism. For instance, the Tahrir party line, developed in the 1950s, still maintains that Britain is the world's hegemonic power. The Ikhwan remains the mainstream and more popular Islamic movement in Jordan. By studying the role of the Ikhwan as political contestants, one can draw conclusions about Islamists' experiences with democracy.

Several factors contribute to the working oppositional relationship between Islamists and the regime in Jordan. One factor lies in the fact that the Hashemite family derives its legitimacy from its claim to descent from the Prophet Muhammad and from its tenure (until expelled by the Saudi family) as guardian of the two holy cities, Makkah and Madinah. The Hashemites consider themselves the legitimate heirs of the Arab Revolt of 1916; as mentioned in Chapter Two, the Arab Revolt contained a strong Islamic element. Being of Prophetic descent, plus bearing the legacy of a politically resistant Islam themselves has given the Hashemites a tricky and vulnerable relationship to modern Islamists. This unique positioning has predisposed the Hashemites to more moderate methods in addressing the Islamists than have been used by other regimes. Even before independence, the government of Transjordan granted license to the Ikhwan to function as an Islamic organization. In 1945, the organization opened its first center in Amman under the auspices of King Abdullah.[22] This was an important symbolic gesture on the King's part indicating Hashemite toleration of the Islamists.

A second reason for the mutually acquiescent relationship between the Jordanian regime and the Muslim Brotherhood is the fact that Islamists rallied around the monarch during several crises, especially those of the 1950s and 1960s and the Civil War. During the first serious challenge to Hussein's crown in 1956, the Jordanian Ikhwan, despite its support for the nationalist agenda of al-Nabulsi's government, sided with the King against what they perceived as a communist threat. The regime's satisfaction with the stand of the Ikhwan led the government to invite them to participate in the 1957 cabinet. The Ikhwan nevertheless turned down the offer, citing the government's lack of commitment to implementing Islam.[23]

Third, Islamists in Jordan conceptualize and define a role for their movement within the boundaries that the regime considers permissible.

According to Islamist leaders, since Jordan lacks the human and material resources to be an ideal Islamic state, and since the regime bases some of its legitimacy on Islam, the movement "does not seek to topple it or replace it with an Islamic regime." Islamists consider the Jordanian regime better than leftist or secular regimes which dominate other Arab countries. They consequently accept for themselves the role of a pressure group which "expresses and defends the values, culture, and civilization of the Muslim community in Jordan."[24]

The Jordanian Islamists' limited objectives, moderate message, and gradual approach has made it possible for them not only to be tolerated, but to be included in the political process. Nevertheless, it was not until 1989 that Islamists had an opportunity to participate on a large scale in Jordanian politics. In that year's election, Islamists rode the wave of popular resentment produced by government corruption, economic crisis, and the absence of political participation, to emerge as the largest winning bloc. Of the twenty-six Islamist candidates running, twenty-two won. Islamist participation in this election contributed to Jordan's democratic experiment in two ways: It gave the process more credibility, since Islamists had been, most of the time, in opposition; and, while serving in parliament, Islamists pushed an agenda of political reform. The representatives of the Islamic movement proved to be flexible and realistic, for the most part, and were able to form coalitions with other political forces. These coalitions worked to Islamist advantage on at least two occasions: when Islamists were able to elect one of themselves as Speaker of Parliament, and when they brought down the cabinet of Tahir al-Misri by denying him a vote of confidence.

Recent Islamist participation in Jordanian politics is characterized by their willingness to join the cabinet of Muder Badran for almost five months in early 1991. The Ikhwan was given five portfolios: education, social development, justice, *awqaf* (Islamic endowments), and health. The main reason for Islamists' abdication of their oppositional role was the accord in which they found themselves with the government over the Gulf Crisis and War. The Jordanian government, as well a majority of the public, sided with Iraq. While their time in government may have been too short to judge their performance as part of the executive branch, they formed a vigorous opposition group in the National Assembly, acting as a watchdog over government activities. Another major concern for Islamists while serving in parliament was to make sure that no legislation disagreed with their understanding of *shari`a*.

The relationship between the Jordanian regime and Islamists has not always been smooth. Every once in a while, the *mukhabarat* remind Islamists and other opposition groups that the government has another side: the stick. In the mid-1980s, the *mukhabarat* engaged in a wide campaign of harassment against political opponents, including Islamists. The usual measures included firing people with ties to the opposition from state-related jobs, confiscating their passports to prevent them from traveling, and occasional arrests. The justification for such measures usually entailed the discovery of a plot to overthrow the regime or an attempt on the life of the King. A recent example was the trial of two members of parliament who identified themselves as independent Islamists (not affiliated with the Ikhwan). The two members, Layth Shubailat and Ya`qub Qirsh, were arrested in 1992, charged with treason and convicted. Two days after their conviction, King Hussein issued an amnesty; they were released and allowed to continue their terms in parliament.[25]

In December 1992, the Ikhwan together with some independent Islamists formed the Islamic Action Front (IAF). The Interior Ministry's licensing of this party and nineteen others, including Ba`thists and communists, was a step toward institutionalizing political pluralism and was appreciated by all political forces in the country. The Islamic Action Front says that its long-term goals include the resumption of Islamic life and the implementation of *shari`a;* the restoration of Palestinian rights; and work toward unifying the Arab nation. The IAF has publicly declared its commitment to democratic practices, pluralism, human rights, and dialogue among all political contenders in Jordan. Its economic platform is based on notions of social justice, private property, equal economic opportunity, and Islamic development and investment.[26] Obvious from these stated goals, from party publications, and from interviews and public statements of Islamist leaders, is a commitment to continue to function within the boundaries set by the regime. The important development embodied by the IAF is that Islamists have entered the political process in a new form, one which requires them to translate their goals into concrete policies, compete with other parties, form coalitions, even take part in government, and, finally, open their ranks to the general public. This is a challenge which Islamists in other Arab countries have not been afforded the opportunity to face.

Near the end of 1992, it became clear that King Hussein was moving toward concluding a peace treaty with Israel, which Islamists adamantly opposed. The government, in anticipation of the difficulty of passing any peace accord with Israel by an Islamist-dominated parliament, amended electoral law so as to reduce the power of the Islamists. Specifically, the amendment allowed voters to vote on only one seat in their district, no matter how many seats are contested. The new electoral law dissipated the power of the voter and virtually disabled a party from electing more than one of its candidates in any single district. The amendment created a situation in which a party's constituency might divide its vote between two of its own candidates, thus giving the advantage to another party's candidate.

Despite protest by almost all political parties and particularly by Islamists, the government passed the amendment. It made sure to slip the amendment through immediately after the dissolution of the previous parliament, which would have overturned this amendment, and shortly before the second parliamentary election of 1993. The Islamists threatened to boycott the election because of this strategy, designed to reduce their representation in the new parliament.[27] They eventually acquiesced to the new rules of the democratic contest and participated in the election anyway.

The Islamic Action Front nominated only thirty-six candidates for the eighty-seat parliament, although it had the option of nominating eighty or even more candidates. According to its Secretary General, IAF strategized this move specifically to avoid a potentially explosive confrontation with the regime over any future deal with Israel.[28] The IAF emerged during the elections as the most disciplined and well-organized party, and secured eighteen seats in the new parliament. Yet because the IAF got fewer seats than it had won in the previous election, its opponents reached a quick conclusion that Islamists were declining in popularity.[29] That contention is fallacious for two reasons: With eighteen seats, the Front emerged as the largest single party in the new parliament, while the other seventeen parties achieved a combined total of only sixteen seats (see Tables 6.2 and 6.3); and the Islamist share of the popular vote (30%) was higher than their proportion of elected representatives (22%). In fact, the number of actual votes they received in the 1993 election was even higher than what they got in 1989.[30] Nevertheless, the resulting parliament was one dominated by progovernment forces.

The King: A Tolerant Monarch Adept at Compromise

King Hussein remains the ultimate arbiter of domestic political life in Jordan and the final decision-maker in foreign policy. As illustrated, he has played the central role in forging a sense of national unity among the inhabitants of Jordan, consolidated a wide network of beneficiaries with high stakes in the survival of the regime; and maintained a moderate and balanced foreign policy orientation which has earned him the respect of the leaders of major powers.

Three traits of Hussein's leadership have been crucial to the unfolding of democracy in Jordan. The first is tolerance. Unlike other Arab leaders, Hussein is known for his leniency toward political critics. This has made him likeable to a large portion of Jordanians, particularly East Bankers. He has distinguished himself by rewarding dissidents with political appointments—even those supposedly engaged in political plots. He has resorted to ruthless measures only on one significant occasion: the 1970 civil conflict which threatened the viability of Jordan and

TABLE 6.2 Political Forces in the 1993 Jordanian Parliament

Affiliation	*Seats*	*Percent*
Islamic Action Front	18	22.5
Independent Islamists	4	5.0
Leftists	2	2.5
Nationalists	9	11.25
Liberals	13	16.25
Pro-government conservatives	34	42.5
Total	80	100

Sources: Al-Sharq al-Awsat, Nov. 21, 1993, p. 5; *Qadaya Dawliyya,* Nov. 22, 1993, p. 5.

TABLE 6.3 Party Returns of Jordan's 1993 Parliamentary Elections

Party	*Candidates*	*Winners*	*Political Affiliation*
Islamic Action Front	36	18	Islamic
Ba`th	5	1	Nationalist
Jordanian National Coalition	4	4	Centrist
Al-`Ahd (Pledge)	4	3	Centrist
Popular Unity	4	0	Leftist
Democratic Populace	4	1	Leftist
Social Democratic	3	1	Leftist
Jordanian Communist	3	0	Leftist
The Awakening	2	2	Centrist
Al-Watan	2	2	Centrist
Al-Mustaqbal (The Future)	2	1	Centrist
Liberty	2	0	Leftist
Du`a'Movement	2	0	Liberal
Democratic Arabic	1	1	Centrist
Jordanian Dem. Progrssive	1	0	Leftist
Progress & Justice	1	0	Centrist
The Party of the Masses	1	0	Leftist
Progressive Ba`th	1	0	Nationalist
Total	78	34	

Source: Compiled from *al-Dustour,* Dec. 5, 1993, p. 11.

his own throne. Even during the absence of parliament from political life, his rule never approached the authoritarianism of the leaders of neighboring Arab countries. Bringing political stability to the country at a relatively low cost in terms of human rights is one achievement Hussein can claim.

A second factor in Hussein's style of leadership relevant to the issue at hand is his ability to rise over internecine political struggles. Hussein relies on the advice of trusted consultants, friends, and family members, most of whom are part of the Royal *Diwan*. He surrounds himself with a few highly loyal individuals and chooses his prime minister from among them while the rest await their turn, mostly as members of the House of Notables. Each man in Hussein's pool of prime ministers is known to favor a policy or an orientation. For instance, Zaid Rifa`i is chosen when the King wants to improve relations with Syria; Zaid bin Shaker, a cousin and former leader of the Army, is known for his firmness during crises; and the conservative Muder Badran has been effective in dealing with domestic forces, especially Islamists. The crowning feature of this style of leadership lies in the fact that when the policy is successful, the King gets credit for it, and when something goes wrong, the prime minister appears conveniently at fault. Thus, when riots broke out in April 1989, people blamed Prime Minister Zaid Rifa`i and not his boss.

Finally, Hussein's penchant for risk-taking has been helpful in the face of his most serious challenges. Moreover, Hussein has shown a tendency to steer a zigzag course both domestically and internationally, sometimes pursuing simultaneously two contradictory policies. While some might consider this conduct opportunistic, Hussein's boldness and ambidexterity in political maneuvering has contributed to his survival in a volatile region. In 1990–1991 he risked opposing the US-led effort to destroy Iraq. Although this position was consistent with Arab public opinion, it ran afoul of the major regional and international powers, and cost him dearly. For the next two years, Jordan lost economic aid from the Gulf states, the United States, and the European community. His willingness to take risks is serviceable in the process of democratization, as evident Hussein's decision to recall parliament and hold free elections after the vehement popular protests against his regime in 1989, many from his own power base in the south.

Hussein's other major step toward democracy was the convening of a committee to form a National Charter. In his speech to the drafters of the Charter, Hussein characterized it as a second stride toward democracy, the first being the parliamentary election. He also wanted to regulate future political activities by building a consensus on what he termed a "social contract."[31] His concern over reaching a consensus was reflected in the composition of the committee: Representatives of all political trends—Islamists, nationalists, communists, Ba`thists, and independents—were included.

The final document, a testament to the art of compromise, prescribes the return of pluralism and other democratic practices as the only viable choice of Jordan, to the satisfaction of oppositional groups; on the other hand, it stresses that Jordan is a legitimate territorial state and the Hashemite dynasty, namely King Hussein, is the legitimate head of that state.[32] Other important articles state that the Jordanian people are part of the Arab nation and Arab unity is the only way to guarantee the security and well-being of the Arab people; that Arabo-Islamic civilization, with its universalist message, is the basis of Jordanian identity; that the state must implement the rule of law and democratic pluralism; and that Islam is the religion of the state and *shari`a* the main source of legislation.

The inclusion of Islam as a central component of Jordan's identity and a source of legislation is the key matter which political forces in other Arab countries are still contesting bitterly. It is the inclusion of this article, an important concession which Islamists in other countries have not been able to achieve, that led Islamists to endorse the Charter. Almost two thousand leaders reflecting diverse elements of Jordanian society responded to the King's invitation to the national conference ratifying the Charter. The National Charter seems to contain the components of a collective identity that can accommodate all the major political players in Jordan. The overwhelming consensus of very nearly all political forces on these principles is a weighty achievement.

To sum up, four factors have combined to make the transition to democracy possible in Jordan. A cluster of socioeconomic factors provided Jordan with the literacy, urbanization, and civic expectations to prepare its citizenry for democracy. Relative prosperity followed by economic crisis provided the immediate motivation for political participation among the masses. Jordanian national identity consolidated in a form acceptable to nearly all political players. The country has a moderate Islamic movement which is willing to work within the political process, together with a political system that is willing to include Islamists, presided over by a shrewd and reasonable king who has managed to survive at a low repressive cost.

Limits and Prospects

The passage of the electoral law amendment before the second parliamentary election, in the absence of a parliament and wide opposition to it among the various political parties, especially Islamists, raises the question of whether the democratic process has reached its limits. While the elections were held as scheduled in November 1993 with all political parties participating, assuring some continuity, this intervention by the regime for the purpose of producing a "friendly" parliament is the first setback. Such manipulation of the democratic process by the regime reflects the overarching defect of Jordanian democratization: The King has placed himself above and outside the entire process. It is true that Hussein increased the scope of political participation, widened the margin of freedom, and legalized political parties, but no mechanism was developed for the transfer of power. On the contrary, the King, in return for these reforms, has reasserted his role as the ultimate arbiter and decision-maker. Thus, the Jordanian democratic case can be characterized as democracy without the transfer of power.

In order for Jordan to move toward genuine democracy it must fulfill two conditions.First, parliament must gain enough power to appoint and change a prime minister and a cabinet based on the criterion of asking the leader of the party with a majority or the largest bloc to form the government. Second, the executive power should belong to the prime minister and his or her cabinet, rather than the king. The cabinet must be accountable before parliament; parliament would carry out the legislative function. In other words, the system of government would become a true constitutional monarchy.

The reality of the current system is that the king has the executive power, aided by a prime minister, advisors, and a cabinet. He has the power to dissolve parliament and dismiss the cabinet. The logical course for further democratization in Jordan is for the King to relinquish gradually some of his power to both parliament and the cabinet. What are the prospects for such a transformation? According to Adam Przeworski, political elites will support democratization only if they believe that their interests will be preserved under the new order.[33] In Jordan, Hussein does not seem to be willing to relinquish his powers very soon. What is more, there are strong forces in Jordanian society with an interest in preserving the Hashemite rule, especially among those who benefit both materially and politically from it. Even those forces who oppose the regime, including Islamists, have not reached the point of working or at least demand the structural changes in the political system at the expense of King Hussein. There are increasing demands among Islamists to empower parliament to carry out its prescribe prerogatives of legislation and oversight of the prime minister and the cabinet.[34] This still does not touch the King.

A second point relevant to the prospect of democracy in Jordan has to do with the role of external forces. The Gulf War demonstrated the conflict between the interests of external powers, especially in "maintaining stability" (read: containing the forces unleashed by democratization). Popular volition bitterly opposed the United States' efforts to impose its hegemony in the Arab world during the Gulf conflict. This is why the countries with some democratic openings, including Jordan, Yemen, Tunisia, Algeria, and Egypt, were the scene of massive protests against the US-led massacre against Iraq. In the Jordanian case, the King sided with his people, expressing strong verbal condemnation of the Western campaign to destroy an Arab country. His position was not appreciated by the United States, Europe, and other Arab allies, and he and his country suffered the consequences. When the Madrid peace talks began, Hussein found a great opportunity to fix the damage done by his stance during the Gulf War. Two years after Madrid, Hussein has signed a peace accord with Israel, something not popular among Jordanians of many political affiliations, but especially Islamists.[35] It seems that this time there is incompatibility in pursuing both goals: peace and democracy. The achievement of peace may be at the expense of suppressing the voices of opposition, which cannot be done democratically. In fact, the undemocratic change in electoral law was the first step toward creating a parliament which would acquiesce to peace with Israel.

King Hussein's reluctance to give up some of his power, the existence of various beneficiaries in Jordanian society, not the least of whom are the chiefs of the Army and the *mukhabarat*, and a preference by the leaders of external powers to deal with Hussein, all make it unlikely that we will witness a transfer of power from the king to parliament and cabinet. And if such possibility is ever to be realized, it is most likely under King Hussein than under whoever may succeed him. Hussein faces the task of reconciling his people to an unequal and unpopular peace with Israel. Since Hussein is the best-positioned to play that role, we will not see Jordan become a full-fledged democratic constitutional monarchy during his reign.

Despite the limitations and flaws in the Jordanian democratic experiment, it is useful in two ways. It provides an alternative to the polarization and violence which characterize the way other Arab regimes have dealt with opposition; and it has succeeded in including Islamists in the political process. It is a model which could be emulated by other Arab regimes, if they changed their perception of Islamists as an unmitigated evil. As for Jordan, a limited exercise of freedom and a partially democratic apparatus is better than nothing. Other democratic experiments in the world have shown that the more freedom people gain, the higher their participatory expectations. These expectations may gather momentum toward a point beyond what the ruler can provide or control.

Notes

1. The first parliamentary election was in 1989.

2. See Chapter 5, Article 93, of the *Constitution of the Hashemite Kingdom of Jordan*.

3. This view is expressed by the King in a press interview published in *Mihnati ka Malik: Ahadith Malakiyya* (My Profession as King: Royal Conversations), trans. from the French by Ghalib Arif Tuqan (Amman: Al-Sharika al-`Arabiyya lil Tiba`a wal Nashr, 1978).

4. An evaluation of this period can be found in Abdul Fatah Rashdan, "Al-Tatawur al Dimoqrati fil Urdun" (Democratic Development in Jordan: 1952–1989), *Qira'at Siyasiyya*, Vol. 4, No. 2, 1994, pp. 94–95.

5. In *Jordan: Crossroads of Middle Eastern Events* (Boulder, CO: Westview Press, 1983), p. 113.

6. Rashdan, "Al-Tatawur . . . ," p. 102.

7. *Middle East International*, Nov. 17, 1989, p. 3.

8. *Keesing's Record of World Events*, Nov., 1989, p. 37052.

9. The literacy rate in Jordan was 80% in 1990; see EIU Country Profile 1994–95, *Jordan* (London: Economist Intelligence Unit, 1994), p. 12.

10. Ibid., p. 11.

11. *Nas al-Mithaq al-Watani al-Urduni* (The Text of the Jordanian National Charter), appendix in Ranad Al-Khatib Ayyad, *al-Tayyarat al-Siyasiyya Fil Urdun* (Political Trends in Jordan) (Amman: al-Matba`a al-Wataniyya, 1991), p. 136.

12. *Keesing's Record of World Events*, April 1989, p. 26602.

13. See, for example, the historical review of Jordan in the "National Charter," Ayyad, *al-Tayyarat*, p. 132.

14. For a recent discussion of the Palestinian impact on Jordan, see Lawrence Tal, "Is Jordan Doomed?" *Foreign Affairs*, Vol. 72, No. 5, 1993, pp. 45–58.

15. "Jordan," *The Middle East and North Africa 1993*, 39th ed. (London: Europa Publications Ltd., 1992), p. 560.

16. *Keesing's Record of World Events*, Nov. 1989, p. 37052.

17. The latter originating in Chechnya.

18. EIU Country Profile 1994–95, *Jordan*, p. 11.

19. In mid-1992, approximately 234.000 Palestinians were still living in refugee camps, and the number of Jordanian citizens who fled from Kuwait to Jordan as a result of the Gulf crisis is estimated around 300.000.

20. Quoted in Tal, "Is Jordan Doomed?" p. 58.

21. This section is based in part on interviews I conducted with the following Islamist leaders and Parliament members in Amman, January 19 to 27, 1993: Dr. Abdullatif Arabiyat, former Speaker of the Parliament; Dr. Abdallah al-Akailah, Parliamentary representative and former Minister of Education; and Dr. Ishaq al-Farhan, former member of the House of Notables and currently Secretary-General of the Islamic Action Front.

22. Awni J. al-Ubaidi, *Jama`at al-Ikhwan al-Muslimin fil Urdun wa Philistine: 1945–1970* (The Muslim Brotherhood Organization in Jordan and Palestine: 1945–1970) (Amman: Al-Maktaba al-Wataniyya, 1991), pp. 36–37. See too, Musa Zaid al-Kailani, *al-Harakat al-Islamiyya fil Urdun* (The Islamic Movements in Jordan) (Amman: Dar al-Bashir, 1990).

23. Ubaidi, ibid., p. 166.

24. Abdallah al-Akailah, "The Experience of the Jordanian Islamic Movement," in Azzam Tamimi, ed., *Power-Sharing Islam?* (London: Liberty for Muslim World Publications, 1993), p. 99.

25. For more illustrations of the regime's use of the "carrot" and the "stick" with Islamists, see Leonard Robinson, "al- Dawla wal Islamiyyun wal Infitah al-Siyasi fil Urdun" (The State, Islamists, and the Political Opening in Jordan), *Qira'at Siyasyyia*, Vol. 4, No. 2, Spring 1994, pp. 33–60.

26. *Hizb Jabhit al-`Amal al-Islami: Al-Nizam al-Asasi* (The Party of the Islamic Action Front: the Bylaws) (Amman: n.p., 1992), pp. 3–9.

27. *Civil Society*, July 1993, p. 18.

28. Personal interview with Ishaq al-Farhan, Islamic Action Front Secretary General, Amman, January 19, 1993.

29. See for instance Y. Ibrahim's article in *New York Times*, Nov. 10, 1993, p. A8, the day after the election, in which he glibly declares that the election was a contest between peace and "fundamentalism," and "fundamentalism" lost.

30. *Al-Dustour* (Jordanian newspaper), Dec. 5, 1993, p. 11.

31. "Kalimat Jalalet al-Malik al-Hussein al-Samiyya ila al-Lajna al-Malakiyya li Siaghat al-Mithaq al-Watani" (Speech of His Majesty King Hussein to the Royal Commission Drafting the National Charter), published as an appendix in Ayyad, *al-Tayyarat*, pp. 119–127.

32. EIU Country Profiles 1994–95, *Jordan*, p. 5.

33. "Democracy as a Contingent Outcome of Conflict," Jon Elster and Rune Stalstad, eds., *Constitutionalism and Democracy* (Cambridge: Cambridge University Press, 1988), p. 79.

34. Ishaq al-Farhan, "al-Islamiyyun wal Masira al-Dimoqratiyya fil Urdun" (Islamists and the Democratic March in Jordan), *Qira'at Siyasiyya*, Vol. 4, No. 2, Spring 1994, p. 118.

35. See for example the statement issued by Islamists and ten other parties and delivered to the Prime Minister, protesting Jordan's commitment to the peace process, in *al-`Amal al- Islami* (Islamic Action), July 10, 1993, p. 9.

PART FOUR

Conclusions

7

Conclusions and Prospects

A wave of democratization pulsed through the Arab world in the 1980s. It did not affect all Arab countries equally, but a significant number of Arab countries experienced the beginnings of democratization. That is, in an exciting transitional phase, the exercise of political power by the state became less arbitrary and exclusive, organized oppositional activities were allowed, freer elections were held, and there was an attempt to open political participation, in some degree, to the masses of people.

Simultaneously, the popularity of Islamists escalated. That is, the number of people who believed that the frame of reference organizing the political (and not just the private) realm could and should be derived from an understanding of the basic texts of Islam increased, and the number of their sympathizers increased. That Islamists had become the most robust opposition to the ruling elites became more apparent with every democratizing measure. To the horror of regimes and Western powers, Islamists won clear victories wherever elections with any modicum of fairness were held.

The rulers responded by putting the brakes on democratization. In Egypt, in Tunisia, in Jordan, electoral laws were busily amended to obstruct Islamist participation. In Egypt and Tunisia, Islamist parties were targeted for exclusion from elections by being denied legal status; the state clamped down its repressive apparatus, harassing and arresting Islamist opposition members. In Algeria, the reversal of democratization peaked when the regime canceled the second round of the parliamentary elections in January 1992 after Islamist landslides in the first round, and acquiesced to a military takeover to preserve the ruling order.

What do these trends mean for democracy in the Arab world? How can they be analyzed without resort to racist and orientalist theories essentializing "Arab" or "Islamic" culture as inimical to democracy? Most importantly, what interpretive lessons can they provide for those committed to the self-determination and well-being of the Arab world and its peoples? Any attempt to answer these questions must involve an understanding of four overlapping issue-clusters in the Arab world: the basic problem of collective identity; socioeconomic challenges; political leadership; and international pressures on the Arab world.

The peoples of the Arab world are still struggling to arrive at a minimal consensus over collective identity. The cohesion of collective identity in the Arab world was damaged by the invasive presence of European powers beginning in the eighteenth century. Even before the rule of Europe over the Islamic heartland occurred, the European onslaught undermined the economy and social stability of those lands. For example, Britain and France had a very conscious policy of "sponsoring" ethnic and religious minorities (the British chose the Druze, for example, and the French chose the Maronites) and planting the seeds of discord in the Arab states they carved out. That "carving out" itself, and colonialism disguised as "mandate" rule, furthered the fragmentation of collective identity among Arabs, creating local statism (*qutriyya*) as an option beside Arab nationalism (*qawmiyya*) after pan-Islamism faded as a viable option. Today, *qutriyya* and *qawmiyya* no longer seem mutually exclusive; Arabs have settled more or less comfortably within local state borders, while at the same time retaining the belief that pan-Arab alliance or confederation is still a viable goal. For although the entities created artificially have grown into Arab states with their own economies, local cultures, and localized combinations of ethnic and sectarian identities; although Nasser's formulation of pan-Arabism foundered; although the Gulf War sharpened certain intra-Arab conflicts; although all this is true, the sense that there is an Arab world remains strong. It is a more complex idea of Arab identity, one that is able to encompass the diversity within the Arab world, that has survived. The new emphasis on Islam, with its universalism and models for the accommodation of diverse religious and ethnic groups, has added to the strength and richness of that sense of Arab identity.

The main question posed in the Arab world today is about the role of Islam in collective identity. The question emerges in two different kinds of states. In states which have generally followed a secularist, "progressive" modernizing program in the postcolonial period (such as Syria, Tunisia, Algeria, Egypt) strong oppositional Islamic movements have mobilized and the two sides have polarized in bitter conflict. Islamists have been perceived as a dire threat by the regimes and have been rendered illegal and excluded from political participation. The conflict over collective identity in these states has accelerated to very extremist positions in both camps. What should make such states move toward democratization is that the two sides are stalemated. The ruling elite lack popularity and legitimacy but controls the state and its security apparatus as well as the valuable resources. The Islamists can mobilize more popular support and are gaining in resources and capability for providing basic services to people which the government fails to provide due to corruption and mismanagement. Neither camp is likely to be able to eradicate the other; neither has a chance for complete victory. This should lead them to rethink their positions. The existence of moderate leadership on both sides who are willing to compromise and to engage in "*hiwar*" (dialogue) is a point in favor of the democratic potential. Why then has authoritarianism not budged much? Authoritarianism in Egypt and Algeria has actually retrenched. This is because the Egyptian regime has not exhausted its "repression option," while the Algerian junta still imagines that it can completely eradicate the Islamists. Extremism and repression on the part of the governments have bred extreme militancy among Islamists and maintains the "zero-sum game" model of politics, which precludes the possibility for negotiation and compromise. Such negotiation and compromise is required for the dynamic of collective identity to reach a point capable of sustaining democracy. Only when both sides acknowledge that violent confrontation will not achieve the change they want will they turn to the *hiwar* option and only then will a politics of inclusion become possible. Democracy has frequently been preceded by civil war.

In states which remained traditional and never pursued a self-consciously secularist program of modernization (such as Jordan, former North Yemen, Kuwait, and some other Gulf states), Islamists have, generally speaking, been allowed to participate in political life and the conflict over collective identity has not been as polarized. In these countries, Islamic movements developed moderate and peaceful ways to work for their political agendas. Rather than being conducted in the arena of violence, the collective identity debate in these nations is generally conducted on the level of national *hiwar*. In Jordan, this negotiation reached a crucial threshold in the National Charter, which represents a new social contract arrived at with the participation of all contenders in the Jordanian political arena. The Islamists of Jordan have been recognized as a legal political party and their agendas have been placed on the negotiating table alongside other agendas. A major prerequisite for democratization has thus been fulfilled in Jordan.

In Saudi Arabia, on the other hand, the ruling family has used its oil profits to evade the whole issue of democratization. By providing all the output services of government, from health care to security, without collecting taxes from its populace, this "rentier state" has silenced all demands for political participation. Even in this state, nonparticipation has begun to be challenged. The Gulf War strained Saudi economic resources, and consequently tested the regime's ability to silence dissent. Disagreement over the moral justification of the War itself created resentment among young Saudis at their total disenfranchisement, resentment which found expression in an activist Islam as opposed to the traditional "blind obedience" Islam of the ruling class. The beginnings of a collective identity debate are taking shape in Saudi Arabia, a debate which is more advanced in Jordan.

Overall in the Arab world, there are encouraging developments on the question of collective identity. There is generally more agreement among intellectuals and leaders of society, ranging from secular nationalists to Islamists, that democracy should not be sacrificed for any cause. Only a few fanatic secularists want Islamists excluded from democracy at any cost. Most would agree with Muhammad Hassanein Heikal in saying, "Personally I am not enthusiastic about the idea of a religious state but nevertheless, if the will of the majority is the source and the basis, and if the majority chooses, then who am I and who are others to have the right to impose upon the masses of people in their democratic choice?" He adds that if Islamists get to power and rule successfully, that is beneficial for the Arab nation; if they get to power and botch things up, so much the better for their opponents. To exclude them from power when they earn it fair and square because of speculation that they will put an end to democracy is hypocritical and dangerous, Heikal concludes.[1] Another indication of support for a democracy which includes Islamists is the Arab Nationalist Convention, which has been held annually since the Gulf War. Influential Arab intellectuals at this gathering recognize the lack of prioritization of democracy as a serious problem in the Arab world. This signalled a change from the position (which was dominant in the 1960s and 1970s) that unity, economic development, and restoration of Palestinian rights must take precedence over democracy. At the fourth meeting (Beirut, May 1993), it was agreed that democracy and dialogue must be inclusive.[2] They proposed the notion of *"al-hiwar al-`arabi al-islami"* (dialogue between Arab nationalists and Islamists). The agreement of nationalists that Islam constitutes a major part of "who we are," regardless of religious affiliation, was an important development toward negotiating consensus on collective identity. Also significant was the fact that Islamists endorsed democracy and pluralism and agreed to work within such a framework, once Islam had been agreed upon as a central component.

Socioeconomic contexts constitute another set of variables. The Arab world can be divided into three clusters according to socioeconomic conditions. There are the oil-producing states with sparse populations and rich resources. There are states with poor resources which may have large populations, such as Egypt (where the GNP per capita is under a thousand dollars), Sudan, Yemen, and Morocco, or may be less populous, such as Mauritania and Somalia. Finally, there are middle-income states:

those with moderate resources (some have oil) but also midsize to large populations, such as Iraq, Algeria, Syria, Jordan, Tunisia, and Lebanon. What does this mean with regard to prospects for democracy?

The inequitable distribution of wealth among and within the countries of the Arab world has contributed to a gap between expectations and actual conditions. It is from these kinds of gaps that transformative change has happened in history. Within many Arab countries, some of whatever wealth the state had was invested in education and infrastructure in the postindependence period, and in the economic expansion of the 1970s. In addition, many Arabs from poorer countries migrated to work in the oil-rich countries, usually sending money back home. These economic developments led to an expansion of the middle classes and the numbers of those with middle-class aspirations, middle-class literacy, and middle-class education. Social and economic change was not, however, accompanied by expansion of the political institutions; the middle classes have not been accommodated in the existing political systems. Economic crisis hit in Egypt, Jordan, Tunisia, Sudan and Algeria (among others) in the 1980s, exacerbating the tensions caused by the political stagnation. Depressed economic conditions at that moment constituted a favorable factor for the beginning of democratization process—because they mobilized discontented masses and forced regimes to liberalize, relieving some of the pressure created by the closed political systems. In the oil-rich "rentier" states, this was postponed until the 1990s, when the cost of the Gulf War finally dented their seemingly inexhaustible financial resources. The Gulf War was estimated to have cost the Saudis and others in the region 676 billion dollars.[3] In 1993–1994, Saudi Arabia had to make a 20 percent cut of expenditures in order to balance its budget. Suddenly the illogic of the complete disenfranchisement of all but the ruling family became apparent to more and more Saudis, and popular discontent, similar to that rising in other Arab countries, began to be heard in the Saudi state, although it was whispered rather than shouted.

Economic conditions are variable in terms of their effect on democracy. It has been observed that most wealthy countries are democracies—but the oil-rich states prove an exception, so far. It has also been observed that most democracies are wealthy—but then India proves even that is not a hard-and-fast correlation. In the Arab world, the effect of economic conditions has varied over time as well as across countries. There are some very poor states in the Arab world, and if poverty is an obstacle to democracy, regional integration would help address the problem of inequitable distribution of resources whose roots lie in the divisions left by colonialism.

External factors that have affected the prospects of democracy are: the legacy of the colonizing powers; the Israeli problem; the Cold War; and the post–Cold War order. Colonialism laid obstacles in the path of any future democratization project by distorting the social cohesion of the Arab world. Israel's presence as a very real security threat in the middle of the Arab world has been used to stifle dissent and justify martial law in Arab countries. Thus, Israel's role has been consistently inimical to democracy in the region. The Cold War was another external factor that worked against the possibility of democratic change in the Arab world. In the competition between the US and the USSR, each side wanted only to gain states as collaborators and to back those states regardless of their authoritarianism. To each camp in the Cold War, the Arab states were producers of oil which they needed to buy and importers of weapons which they needed to sell. The policies of the superpowers were designed to keep the oil flowing, the arms market booming, and stability—defined largely in terms of these two elements—intact. Militarization helped Arab regimes to control and repress more efficiently; strong militaries were used both against foreign enemies and frequently to quell domestic strife. The security apparatus of most Arab states, notably the secret police or *mukhabarat*, expanded rapidly in such an encouraging world environment.

As the Cold War drew to a close, the crumbling of authoritarian regimes in the Eastern bloc had a thrilling demonstrative effect on Arab people. Seeing the authoritarian Ceaucescu, who had been a friend of many Arab rulers, meet his end, gave Arab populations the empowering sense that their turn was at hand. Then came the Gulf War. The United States, leader of the post–Cold War era, let loose its massive firepower to ravage Iraq's military capabilities. Once again, the Arab world got the message that keeping the oil flowing to the world powers was more important than the self-determination of Arab peoples. Whatever else had changed in the "new world order," that much was constant. "The Gulf Crisis . . . was an intervention in the name of human rights and global order that, at least in the short term, turned out to be a defense of the most traditional and least representative regimes in the Middle East, or indeed, the world."[4] To make its indifference to democracy even more clear, the United States did nothing to support the uprising of Kurds and Shi`ites in Iraq. An even more blatant indication of the meaning of the "new world order" was the US embrace of Syria's Asad, authoritarian par excellence, into this new order because he supported the US-led coalition against Iraq. All was to be subordinated to preserving the status quo ante of the Gulf War. Another negative role played by the international community is the silence, complicity, and relief with which Algeria's military coup was welcomed in France, the European community, and even the United States. The coup, and the absence of international outrage or pressure against it, was a major blow to democracy in the Arab world.

Then there is the Middle East peace process. Theoretically, Arab peace with Israel should have a positive influence on the prospects for democracy since it would deprive regimes of the excuse that it is necessary to suppress internal dissent in order to defend against the Israeli threat. The catch is that the majority of politically active Arabs do not support it. Israel has signed treaties with regimes that are struggling to stay in power; the most popular forces contesting to gain power, Islamists, were not included in the negotiations. Jordan may perhaps be a test case for the viability of such a "peace." Thus far, Islamists have been included and integrated in Jordanian politics. Jordanian Islamists, like other Islamists, oppose the current peace deal as unjust to the Palestinians. Will democracy in Jordan be subordinated to the external pressures from Israel and the United States? Will Jordan be constrained to suppress its Islamists to meet the terms of a peace lacking a popular mandate?

International support for democracy has led to positive developments elsewhere. At least such support legitimizes the struggle of groups within a particular country who seek enfranchisement and may help rulers see that it is in their interest to allow some democratic measures to take place. The United States has pressured regimes from Kampuchea to Cuba to implement democratic measures. At the 1991 Arab-Israeli peace conference in Madrid, "one word was conspicuously absent amid President Bush's resounding rhetoric about a better future for the Middle East. The missing word was 'democracy' . . . Some were troubled that in such an important setting the US leader did not offer a long-term vision of democracy as a concept that might truly stabilize the troubled Middle East."[5] The European Community and the United States have played a role in encouraging Eastern European states to democratize and rewarding those that did. Major powers and international institutions have played a positive role in encouraging democracy in other parts of the world. Only the Arab world has been overlooked amid solicitous international concern for democracy.

Political leadership is a fourth element. Imaginative, flexible leadership is required for democratization to continue and to produce results; leadership that is hostile to the notion of democratic change can do considerable damage to the whole process. Generally, ruling elites in Arab countries have neither commitment to democracy nor self-motivation for political change. Asad, Qaddafi, and Saddam Hussein, recently joined by Mubarak, are leaders whose hold on power is tenacious, immoderate, and uncompromising. Jordan's Hussein certainly does not want to step down from power, but has shown more willingness to compromise, perhaps to move toward constitutional monarchy. Democratization in the Gulf states could come about following the Jordanian model, through rulers giving more power to elected bodies. On the bright side, all these leaders are in their sixties among a people whose male life expectancy averages between sixty and seventy years. Sometimes a change in leadership is a prerequisite for democratic change.

As far as political leadership among the Islamist opposition, there is a more diverse pool of leaders and leadership qualities. The Ikhwan (Muslim Brotherhood) in Egypt, however moderate, suffers from leadership with tired, obsolete ideas; there is a generation gap between the leadership and the rank-and-file. Jordan's Islamic Alliance, on the other hand, has a diverse and rotating set of leaders, which increases its ability to respond to the changing concerns of its constituency and provide fresh vision. The biggest challenge facing the leadership is how to keep hardliners in each camp from sabotaging what prospects for democratization exist.

If we consider all the factors encouraging democratization—collective identity resolution, favorable socioeconomic conditions, helpful external influences, and skillful political leadership—it is apparent that no Arab country combines all of them; none is without serious impediments to democracy. Still, the crucial factor, which would at least prevent further deterioration of political cohesion, is the inclusion of Islamists in the political process.

> If secular governments in the Middle East want to avoid the problems facing regimes in Egypt and Algeria, where religious extremists have stepped up violent attacks on government officials and others, they should allow Islamist forces to participate fully in the democratic process. Instead of realizing their worst fears, secular leaders may find that such participation might moderate Islamists' behavior and defuse the tensions that have given rise to religiously-inspired political agitation in the region.[6]

Jordan's experiment is successful in that respect. Other countries which have recognized and included Islamists are Yemen, Kuwait, and Lebanon. Governments in these countries should be prepared to accept power-sharing, first in legislative bodies, and eventually, in the alternation of executive power. Islamists in these countries have so far shown an adequate capacity for working within a system that requires sharing and rotation of power. The peaceful transfer of power at the executive level is the next step, the point at which the extent of a polity's democratization is tested and becomes habitual.

The Arab world is experiencing the beginning of a struggle for wider participation in political decision-making. Masses of people are demanding inclusion, enfranchisement, empowerment, directly challenging the hoarding of power by tiny elites, clans, families, military juntas. Under ideal circumstances, the logical end of such a struggle would be the transformation of authoritarian systems into democratic ones.

Because there are so many obstacles to democratization from within and from outside the process of this struggle, it may work itself out in another direction. Authoritarianism may continue. Authoritarianism in some Arab states today has not exhausted its repressive options, but it is different from the authoritarianism of the past: On the level of intellectual debate, hardly anyone is left who maintains that democracy is an unauthentic foreign concept or a deferrable luxury that should take a back seat to more urgent goals. And on the level of practice, there are now many grass-roots movements resisting the authoritarian order.

Besides democratization and the continuation of present authoritarian regimes, there is a third possibility. In the face of the current regimes' resolve to tighten repression, violent change instigated by populist forces is a very real possibility. Such a revolution is not likely to result in a democratic state. It may bring to power populist Islamist forces which would form a new radical authoritarian state.

Two final observations. Authoritarianism is not the only problem enervating the Arab world: The unjust distribution of resources both within and among countries, local and regional disputes, underdevelopment, and dependency on the North, require new solutions. There is widespread agreement that democracy cannot be sacrificed in the name of these goals any longer. A higher level of inter-Arab coordination and integration must take place. Such economic and social pooling of resources among Arab populations is a good which would require and foster higher levels of democratic practice in Arab countries.

Finally, if democracy comes to the Arab world, it may not produce policy content supportive of Western interests. By definition, democracy is the right of the people to choose how they will rule themselves. This choice cannot but emerge from agreements painstakingly arrived at between the people of the polity itself, based on their understanding of the world, of government and what they want it to do, of who they are and who they want to be.

Notes

1. "Muhammad Hassanein Heikal fi Hiwar ma` Phillip Jallab," (Muhammad Hassanein Heikal in a Dialogue with Phillip Jallab), *al- 'Ahali*, Jan. 29, 1992, p. 3 and P. 10.

2. "Al-Mu'tamar al-Qawmi al-Rabi`: Bayan ila al-Umma" (The Fourth National Convention: A Statement to the Nation), *al- Mustaqbal al-`Arabi*, No. 174, June 1993, pp. 141–161.

3. Youssef M. Ibrahim, "Gulf War Is Said to Have Cost the Region $676 Billion in 1990–91," *New York Times*, April, 25, 1993, p. 14.

4. Dankwart Rustow,"The Gulf War and the Future Global (and Arab?) Order," in Stanley Renshon, ed., *The Political Psychology of The Gulf War* (Pittsburgh, PA: University of Pittsburgh Press, 1993), p. 323.

5. Gerald F. Seif, *The Wall Street Journal*, Nov. 4, 1991.

6. Joyce Davis," Islamists and Secular Regimes: Is Violence Inevitable?" *Special Report*, Washington DC: United States Institute of Peace, February, 1994, p. 1.

Bibliography

English

Abdallah, Ahmad. "Egypt's Islamists and the State: From Complicity to Confrontation." *Middle East Report.* (July–Aug. 1993): 29–31.

Abdallah, Umar. *The Islamic Struggle in Syria.* Berkeley, CA: Mezan Press, 1984.

Abdel Khalek, Gouda. "The Open Door Economic Policy in Egypt: Its Contribution to Investment and its Equity Implications," in M. Keer & E. Yassin, eds., *Rich and Poor States in the Middle East: Egypt and the New Arab Order.* Boulder, CO: Westview Press, 1982, pp. 259–283.

Abrahamian, Ervand. *Khomeinism: Essays on the Islamic Republic.* Berkeley, CA: University of California Press, 1993.

AbuKhalil, As'ad. "A New Arab Ideology?: The Rejuvenation of Arab Nationalism." *Middle East Journal.* Vol. 46, No. 1 (1992): 22–36.

Affendi, Abdulwahab el-. "Studying My Movement: Social Science Without Cynicism." *International Journal of Middle East Studies.* Vol. 23, No. 1 (1991): 83–94.

______. *Turabi's Revolution: Islam and Power in Sudan.* London: Grey Seal Books, 1991.

Akailah, Abdallah, al-. "The Experience of the Jordanian Islamic Movement." In Azzam Tamimi, ed., *Power-Sharing Islam?* London: Liberty for Muslim World Publications, 1993, pp. 93–101.

Almond, Gabriel A. and Sydney Verba. *The Civic Culture.* Princeton, NJ: Princeton University Press, 1963.

Anderson, Lisa. "Democracy in the Arab World: A Critique of the Political Culture Approach." Paper delivered at the Conference on Political Liberalization and Democratization in the Arab World. McGill University, May 7–8, 1993.

Antonius, George. *The Arab Awakening.* New York, NY: Capricorn, 1945.

Awa, Muhammad S., el-. *On the Political System of the Islamic State.* Indianapolis, IN: American Trust Publications, 1980.

Banks, Arthur, ed. *Political Handbook of the World, 1991.* Binghamton, NY: SUNY University, 1991.

Banna, Hasan al. *Six Tracts of Hasan al-Banna.* Kuwait: International Islamic Federation of Student Organizations, n.d.

Barakat, Halim. *The Arab World: Society, Culture, and State.* Berkeley, CA: University of California Press, 1993.

Ben Eissa, Rachid. "The Algerian Experiment." In Azzam Tamimi, ed., *Power-Sharing Islam?* London: Liberty for Muslim World Publications, 1993, pp. 141–144.

Boustani, Rafic and Philippe Fargues. *The Atlas of the Arab World*. New York, NY: Facts on File, 1991.

Brown, Bernard E. and Roy C. Macridis. *Comparative Politics: Notes and Readings*. 7th ed. Pacific Grove, CA: Brooks/Cole, 1990.

Brown, L. Carl. *International Politics and the Middle East*.

Princeton, NJ: Princeton University Press, 1984.

The Hashemite Kingdom of Jordan. *Constitution of the Hashemite Kingdom of Jordan*. Amman, n.d.

Dahl, Robert A. *Polyarchy: Participation and Opposition*. New Haven, CT: Yale Universiy Press, 1971.

Davis, Joyce. "Islamists and Secular Regimes: Is Violence Inevitable?" *Special Report*. Washington, DC: United States Institute of Peace, 1994. No pagination.

Diamond, Larry, Juan Linz, and Seymour M. Lipset, eds. *Democracy in Developing Countries*. Vol. 3: *Asia*. Boulder, CO: Lynne Reinner, 1989.

Duri, 'Abd al-'Aziz. *The Historical Formation of the Arab Nation*, trans. Lawrence I. Conrad. New York, NY: Croom Helm, 1987.

EIU Country Profile 1994/95. *Egypt*. London: The Economist Intelligence Unit, 1994.

EIU Country Profile 1994/95. *Jordan*. London: The Economist Intelligence Unit, 1994.

EIU Country Report 3rd Quarter 1994. *Egypt*. London: The Economist Intelligence Unit, 1994.

Entelis, John P. and Phillip C. Naylor, eds. *State and Society in Algeria*. Boulder, CO: Westview Press, 1992.

Erian, Essam, al-. "The Future of Power-Sharing in Egypt," in Azzam Tamimi, ed., *Power-Sharing Islam?* London: Liberty for Muslim World Publications, 1993, pp. 159–168.

Esposito, John. "Presidential Address 1989. The Study of Islam: Challenges and Prospects." *Middle East Studies Association Bulletin*, Vol. 24 (1990): 1–11.

______. *Islam: The Straight Path*. New York: Oxford University Press, 1991.

______. *The Islamic Threat*. New York: Oxford University Press, 1992.

Esposito, John and James Piscatori. "Democratization and Islam." *Middle East Journal*, Vol. 45 (Summer 1991): 427–440.

Fukuyama, Francis. "The End of History?" *National Interest*, (Summer 1989): 3–18.

______. "Liberal Democracy as a Global Phenomenon." *PS: Political Science & Politics*, (Dec. 1991): 659–664.

Fuller, Graham E. *The Democracy Trap*. New York, NY: Dutton Books, 1991.

Gubser, Peter. *Jordan: Crossroads of Middle Eastern Events*. Boulder, CO: Westview Press, 1983.

Haddad, Yvonne. "The Arab-Israeli Wars, Nasserism, and the Affirmation of Islamic Identity." In J. Esposito, ed., *Islam and Development*. Syracuse, NY: Syracuse University Press, 1980, pp. 107–121.

Hedges, Chris. "As Egypt Votes on Mubarak, He Faces Rising Peril." *New York Times*. October 13, 1993.

______. "Egypt Begins Crackdown on Strongest Opposition Groups." *New York Times*. June 12, 1994.

Heikal, Mohamed. *Autumn of Fury: The Assassination of Sadat*. New York, NY: Random House, 1983.
______. *Illusions of Triumph: An Arab View of the Gulf War*. London: Harper Collins Publishers, 1992.
Hourani, Albert. *Arab Thought in the Liberal Age: 1798–1939*. Oxford: Oxford University Press, 1962.
______. *The History of the Arab Peoples*. Cambridge, MA: Belknap Press of Harvard University, 1991.
Hudson, Michael. "Presidential Address 1987: Democratization and the Problem of Legitimacy in Middle East Politics." *Middle East Studies Association Bulletin*. Vol. 22, No. 2 (Dec. 1988): 157–171.
______. "After the Gulf War: Prospects for Democratization in the Arab World." *Middle East Journal*. Vol. 45 (Summer 1991): 407–426.
Hunter, Shireen. *The Politics of Islamic Revivalism*. Bloomington, IN: Indiana University Press, 1988.
Huntington, Samuel. "Will More Countries Become Democratic?" *Political Science Quarterly*, Vol. 99, No. 2 (Summer 1984): 193–218.
______. "The Modest Meaning of Democracy." In Robert A. Pastor, ed., *Democracy in the Americas*. New York, NY: Holmes & Meier, 1989, pp. 11–28.
______. *The Third Wave: Democratization in the Late Twentieth Century*. Norman, OK: University of Oklahoma Press, 1991.
______. "Democracy's Third Wave." *Journal of Democracy*, Vol. 2, No. 2 (1992): 12–34.
Hussaini, Ishak M. *The Muslim Brethren: The Greatest of Modern Islamic Movements*. Beirut: Khayat's College Book, 1956.
Ibrahim, Saad Eddin. "Crises, Elites, and Democratization in the Arab World." *Middle East Journal*, Vol. 47, No. 2 (Spring 1993): 292–305.
______. "Egypt's Islamic Militants." *MERIP Reports*, (Feb. 1982): 5–18.
Ibrahim, Youssef M. "Gulf War Is Said to Have Cost the Region $676 Billion in 1990–91." *New York Times*, April 25, 1993, p. 14.
Kaplan, Robert. "Eaten From Within." *Atlantic Monthly*, November, 1994.
Kedourie, Elie. *Democracy and Arab Political Culture*. Washington DC: The Washington Institute for Near East Policy, 1992.
Kramer, Gudrun. "Liberalization and Democracy in the Arab World." *Middle East Report*, (January–Feb. 1992): 22–25.
______. "Islamist Notions of Democracy," *Middle East Report*, (July–Aug. 1993): 2–8.
Lenczowski, George. *The Political Awakening in the Middle East*. Englewood Cliffs, NJ: Prentice-Hall, 1970.
Linz, Juan J. and Alfred Stepan, eds. *The Breakdown of Democratic Regimes*. Baltimore, MD: The Johns Hopkins University Press, 1978.
Lipset, Seymour M. "Some Social Requisites of Democracy: Economic Development and Political Legitimacy." *American Political Science Review*, Vol. 53, No. 1 (1959): 69–105.
Lowry, Arthur, ed. *Islam, Democracy, the State and the West: A Round Table with Dr. Hasan Turabi*. WISE Monograph Series #1. Tampa, FL: World and Islam Studies Enterprise, 1993.

Makram Ebeid, Mona. "The Role of Official Opposition," in Charles Tripp and Roger Owen, eds., *Egypt Under Mubarak*. London: Routledge, 1987, pp. 21–52.

The Middle East and North Africa 1993, 39th ed. London: Europa Publications Ltd., 1992.

Miller, Judith. "The Islamic Wave." *The New York Times Magazine*, May 31, 1992, pp. 22–42.

The Movement of Islamic Tendency in Tunisia: The Facts. Tunis: Movement of Islamic Tendency, 1987.

Nasser, Gamal Abdul. *Egypt's Liberation: The Philosophy of the Revolution*. Washington, DC: Public Affairs Press, 1955.

Norton, Augustus Richard. "The Future of Civil Society in the Middle East." *Middle East Journal*. Vol. 47, No. 2 (Spring 1993): 203–216.

O'Donnell, Guillermo. *Modernization and Bureaucratic Authoritarianism*. Berkeley, CA: University of California Press, 1973.

Patai, Raphael. *The Arab Mind*. New York, NY: Charles Scribner's Sons, 1973.

The Political Program of the Islamic Salvation Front. Algeria: Islamic Salvation Front, 1990.

Pryce-Jones, David. *The Closed Circle: An Interpretation of the Arabs*. New York, NY: Harper & Row, 1989.

Przeworski, Adam. "Democracy as a Contingent Outcome of Conflict." In Jon Elster and Rune Stalstad, eds., *Constitutionalism and Democracy*. Cambridge: Cambridge University Press, 1988, pp. 59–81.

Pye, Lucian. "Political Culture Revisited." *Political Psychology*. Vol. 12, No. 3 (1991): 487–508.

Qaradawi, Yusuf, al-. *Islamic Awakening Between Rejection and Extremism*. Herndon, VA: International Institute of Islamic Thought and American Trust Publications, n.d.

Razi, G. Hossein. "Legitimacy, Religion, and Nationalism in the Middle East." *American Political Science Review*. Vol. 1, No. 1 (Mar. 1990): 69–92.

Rustow, Dankwart. *A World of Nations: Problems of Political Modernization*. Washington DC: Brooking's Institute, 1967.

______. "Nation." In. David Sills, ed., *International Encyclopedia of the Social Sciences*. Vol. 2. New York, NY: MacMillan/Free Press, 1969, pp. 7–14.

______. "The Political Impact of the West." In P.M. Holt, A.K.S. Lambton, and Bernard Lewis, eds., *The Cambridge History of Islam*. Cambridge: Cambridge University, 1970. Vol. 1, pp. 673–697.

______. "Transition to Democracy: Toward a Dynamic Model." *Comparative Politics*, No. 2 (April 1970): 337–365.

______. "Elections and Legitimacy in the Middle East." *The Annals of the American Academy*. Vol. 482, (Nov. 1985): 122–146.

______. "Democracy: A Global Revolution?" *Foreign Affairs*, Vol. 69, No. 4 (1990): 75–91.

______. "Dictatorship to Democracy: The Political Transition." Development Study Programme Roundtable on Global Change. Bucharest: United Nations Development Programme, 1992.

______. "Arab Perceptions of History and the Question of Identity." In Stanley Renshon, ed., *The Political Psychology of the Gulf War*. Pittsburgh, PA: University of Pittsburgh, 1993, pp. 23–26.

______. "The Gulf War and the Future Global (and Arab?) Order." In Stanley A. Renshon, ed., *The Political Psychology of the Gulf War*. Pittsburgh, PA: University of Pittsburgh, 1993, pp. 317–325.

Rustow, Dankwart and Kenneth P. Erickson, eds., *Comparative Political Dynamics: Global Research Perspectives*. New York, NY: Harper Collins, 1991.

Sadat, Anwar. *In Search of Identity: An Autobiography*. New York, NY: Harper & Row, 1978.

Said, Edward. "The Phony Islamic Threat." *New York Times Magazine*, November 21, 1993, pp. 62–64.

Schumpeter, J.A. *Capitalism, Socialism, and Democracy*. 2nd ed. New York, NY: Harper, 1947.

Seale, Patrick. *The Struggle for Syria: A Study of Post-War Arab Politics*. London: Oxford University Press, 1965.

Seif, Gerald F. *Wall Street Journal*, Nov. 4, 1991.

Shaalan, Mohammed. "Political-Psychological Influences in Islamic Revivalist Movements." *Political Psychology*, Vol.7, No. 4 (1986): 811–816.

Sharabi, Hisham. *Arab Intellectuals and the West: The Formative Years 1875–1914*. Baltimore, MD: Johns Hopkins, 1970.

Sorensen, George. *Democracy and Democratization*. Boulder, CO: Westview Press, 1993.

Tal, Lawrence. "Is Jordan Doomed?" *Foreign Affairs*, Vol. 72, No. 5 (1993): 45–58.

Wesson, Robert, ed. *Democracy: A World Survey*. New York, NY: Praeger, 1987.

Wickham, Carrie R. "Beyond Democratization: Political Change in the Arab World." *PS Political Science and Politics*, Vol. 27, No. 3 (1994): 507–509.

Wright, Robin. "Islam, Democracy, and the West." *Foreign Affairs*, Vol. 71, No. 3 (1992): 131–145.

Arabic

Abdallah, Ismael S. et al, eds. *Al-Harakat al-Islamiyya al- Mu`asera fil Watan al-`Arabi* (The Contemporary Islamic Movements in the Arab World). Lebanon: Markaz Dirasat al-Wahda al-`Arabia, 1987.

Ahmed, Rafa`t Said. *Limaza Qatalu al-Sadat: Qisat Tanzim al-Jihad* (Why They Killed Sadat: The Story of the al-Jihad Organization). Cairo: Dar al-Sharqiyya, 1989.

______. *Tanzimat al-Ghadab al-Islami fi al-Sab`inat* (The Organizations of Islamic Rage in the 1970s). Cairo: Maktabat Madbuli, 1989.

______. "Al-Islamiyun: Al-Sulta wal `Unf (Islamists: Power and Violence). *Middle East Affairs Journal*, Vol. 2, No. 1 (1994): 71–82.

Akef, Mahmud and Muhammad Ghurab, eds. *Al-Umma fi Amm: Taqrir Hawli An al-Shu'oon al-Siyasiyya wal Iqtisadiyya al-Masriyya* (The Nation in a Year: An Annual Report on Egyptian Political and Economic Affairs). Cairo: Umma Press and al-Istishariyuun al-`Arab, 1991.

Akef, Mahmud, ed. *Al-Umma fi Amm 1991–1992* (The Nation in a Year: 1991–1992). Cairo: Markaz al-Dirasat al-Hadariyya, 1992.

Ayyad, Ranad K. *Al-Tayyarat al-Siyasiyya Fil Urdun* (Political Trends in Jordan). Amman: Al-Matba`a al-Wataniyya, 1991.

Banna, Hassan al-. *Majmu`at Rasa'il al-Imam al-Shahid Hassan al Banna* (The Collected Letters of the Martyred Imam Hassan al Banna). Beirut: al-Mu'assassa al- Islamiyya, 1981.

Bayan min al-Ikhwan al-Muslimin Hawla Mawjat al-Unf wal Irhab (Communique from the Muslim Brotherhood about the Wave of Violence and Terrorism). Cairo: March 3, 1993.

Burnamij al-Intikhabi li Murashahi Jama`at al-Ikhwan al- Muslimin, al-. (Electoral Program of Muslim Brotherhood Candidates in Jordan). Pamphlet. Amman, 1989.

Cantori, Louis. "Al-Muhafaza wal Taqadum fi Misr: Al-Ihya' al-Islami" (Conservatism and Progressivism in Egypt: The Islamic Revival). Trans. staff. *Qira'at Siyassiyya*, Vol. 3, No. 2 (Spring 1993): 8–26.

Faraj, Abd al-Salam. "Al-Farida al-Gha'iba" (The Forgotten Obligation). Appendix in Ni`mallah Junaina, *Tanzim al-Jihad* (The Jihad Organization). Cairo: Dar al-Hurriyya, 1988.

Farhan, Ishaq, al-. "Al-Islamiyuun wal Masira al-Dimoqratiyya Fil Urdun" (Islamists and the Democratic March in Jordan). *Qira'at Siyasiyya*, Vol. 4, No. 2 (1994): 115–126.

Ghannouchi, Rashid, al-. *Al-Mar'a Bain al-Qur'an wa Waqi` al-Muslimin* (Woman Between the Qur'an and the Reality of Muslims). Tunisia: Matba`at Tunis, n.d.

______. "Al-Dimoqratiyya wal Wad` al-Tunisi" (Democracy and the Tunisian Situation). *Al-Insan*, No. 8 (Aug. 1992): 57–69.

______. *Al-Huriyat al-`Amma fil Dawla al-Islamiyya* (Public Liberties in the Islamic State). Beirut: Markaz Dirasat al-Wahda al-`Arabia, 1993.

______. Huquq al-Muwatana: *Huquq Ghair al-Muslimin fil Mujtama` al-Islami* (The Rights of Citizenship: The Rights of Non-Muslims in the Islamic Society). 2nd ed. Herndon: International Institute of Islamic Thought, 1993.

Ghazali, Muhammad, al-. *Al-Islam wal Istibdad al-Siyasi* (Islam and Political Despotism). Cairo: n.p., 1949.

______. *Al-Sunna al-Nabawiyya Baina Ahl al-Fiqh wa Ahl al-Hadith* (The Prophetic Tradition Between Fiqh Scholars and Hadith Scholars.) Lebanon: Dar al-Shuruq, 1989.

Halima, Abd al-Mun`im M. *Hukm al-Islam fil Dimoqratiyya* (Islam's Judgement on Democracy). Amman: Al-Sharika al-Jadida, 1993.

Hamdan, Gamal. *Shakhsiyyat Misr: Dirasa fi Abqariyat al-Makan* (Egypt's Personality: A Study in the Genius of the Place). Cairo: Maktabat al-Nahda al-Misriyya, 1970.

Haraka al-Dusturiyya al-Islamiyya fil Kuwait, al- (The Islamic Constitutional Movement in Kuwait). Kuwait: n.p., 1991.

Hizb Jabhat al-`Amal al-Islami: Al-Nizam al-Asasi (The Party of the Islamic Action Front: Bylaws). Amman: n.p., 1992.

Hussain, Adel, and Hilmi Murad. *Limaza Naqul La Fi Istitla` al-Ri'asa al-Qadima* (Why We Say No to the Coming Presidential Referendum). Cairo: Labor Party, 1993.

Hussein bin Talal, King of Jordan. *Mihnati ka Malik: Ahadith Malakiyya* (My Profession as King: Royal Conversations). Trans. Ghalib Arif Tuqan. Amman: Al-Sharika al-`Arabia lil Tiba`a wal Nashr, 1978.

Huwaidi, Fahmi. "Al-Islam wal Dimoqratiyya" (Islam and Democracy). *Al-Mustaqbal al-`Arabi*, No. 166 (December 1992): 4–37.

______. "Ijhad al-Hulm al-Dimoqrati fi Misr" (The Abortion of the Democratic Dream in Egypt). *Qira'at Siyasiyyah,* Vol. 7, No. 3 (1994): 139–145.

Ibrahim, Saad Eddin. *Al-Mujtama` wal Dawla fil Watan al-`Arabi* (Society and State in the Arab World). Lebanon: Markaz Dirasat al-Wahda al-`Arabia, 1988.

______, ed. *Al-Ta`adudiyya al-Siyasiyya wal Dimoqratiyya fil Watan al-`Arabi.* (Political Pluralism and Democracy in the Arab World). Amman: Muntada al-Fikr al-`Arabi, 1989.

Junaina, Ni`mallah. *Tanzim al-Jihad* (The Jihad Organization). Cairo: Dar al-Hurriyya, 1988.

Kailani, Musa Zaid al-. *Al-Harakat al-Islamiyya fil Urdun* (The Islamic Movements in Jordan). Amman: Dar al-Bashir, 1990.

Kawakibi, Abdurahman. *Taba'i` al-Istibdad wa masari` al-Isti`bad* (The Characteristics of Tyranny and the Crimes of Oppression). Cairo: n.p, n.d.

Khalidi, Mahmud. *Qawa`ed Nizam al-Hukm fil Islam.* (Principles of the Political System in Islam). Kuwait: Dar al-Buhuth al-`Ilmiyya, 1980.

Krar, Muhammad Ahmad. *Intikhabat wa Barlamanat al-Sudan* (The Elections and Parliaments of Sudan). Khartoum: Institute of Research and Social Studies, 1989.

Mithaq Harakat al-Muqawama al-Islamiyya fi Philistine (The Covenant of the Islamic Resistance Movements in Palestine.) Palestine: Hamas, 1988.

Mithaq al-Jabha al-Qawmiyya al-Islamiyya (Constitution of the Islamic National Front). Sudan: Islamic National Front, n.d.

Muhakamat al-Nizam al-Siyasi (Trials of the Political System). Cairo: Al-Gama`a al-Islamiyya, n.d.

"Mujaz `An al-Shura fil Islam wa Ta`adud al-Hizbi fil Mujtama` al-Muslim" (A Brief on Consultation in Islam and Party Pluralism in Muslim Society). *Resolutions and Recommendations Issued by the International Organization of the Muslim Brotherhood.* Pamphlet. Cairo: March 1994.

Nefeisi, Abdullah, ed. *Al-Haraka al-Islamiyya: Ru'ya Mustaqbaliyya.* (The Islamic Movement: A Forward Vision). Cairo: Madbouli, 1989.

Qaradawi, Yusuf, al-. "Al-Itar al-`Am lil Sahwa al-Islamiyya al-Mu`asera" (The General Framework of the Contemporary Islamic Resurgence). In Saad Eddin Ibrahim, ed. *Al-Sahwa al-Islamiyya wa Humum al-Watan al-`Arabi* (The Islamic Resurgence and the Concerns of the Arab World). Amman: Muntada al-Fikr al-`Arabi, 1988, pp. 15–114.

______. *Fatawa Mu`asera* (Contemporary *Fatwas*). Vol 2. Cairo: Dar al-Wafa', 1993.

Qutb, Muhammad. *Jahiliyyat al-Qarn al-`Ishrin* (The Twentieth Century Ignorance). Beirut: Dar al-Shuruq, 1978.

Qutb, Sayyid. *Ma`alim `ala al-Tariq* (Milestones on the Path). Cairo: Dar al-Shuruq, 1982.

Radi, Mohsen, ed. *Al-Ikhwan Tahta Qubat al-Barlaman* (The Ikhwan Under the Parliamentary Rotunda). Cairo: Dar al-Tawzi` wal Nashr al-Islamiyya, 1990.

Rashdan, Abdul Fatah. "Al-Tatawur al Dimoqrati fil Urdun" (Democratic Development in Jordan: 1952–1989). *Qira'at Siyasiyya*, Vol. 4, No. 2 (1994): 81–114.

Rayis, Muhammad Diya' al-Din, al-. *Al-Nazariyat al-Siyasiyya al-Islamiyya* (Islamic Political Theories), 3rd ed. Cairo: Anglo-Egyptian Library, 1960.

Robinson, Leonard. "Al-Dawla wal Islamiyun wal Infitah al-Siyasi fil Urdun" (The State, Islamists, and the Political Opening in Jordan). Trans. staff. *Qira'at Siyasiyya*, Vol. 4, No. 2 (Spring 1994): 33–60.

Sabuni, Abdurahman, al-. "Muhadarat fi Nizam al-Hukm fil Islam" ("Lectures on the Political System in Islam"), unpublished papers. United Arab Emirates: Sharia and Law College, U.A.E. University, 1983.

Salame, Ghassan. "Halat al-Ta`adudiyya al Siyasiyya fi al- Mashriq al-`Arabi" (The Status of Political Pluralism in the Arabic East). In *Al-Ta`adudiyya al-Siyasiyya wal Dimoqratiyya fil Watan al-`Arabi* (Political Pluralism and Democracy in the Arab World). Amman: Muntada al-Fikr al- `Arabi, 1989, pp. 141–152.

Sarhal, Ahmed. *Al-Nuzm al-Siyasiyya wal Dustouriyya fi Lubnan wal Duwal al-`Arabia* (The Political and Constitutional Systems in Lebanon and the Arab States). Beirut: Dar al-Bahith, 1980.

Sharif, Kamel al-. *Al-Ikhwan al-Muslimun fi Harb Philistine* (The Muslim Brotherhood in the Palestine War). Cairo: Maktabat Wahba, n.d.

______. *Al Muqawamma al-Sirriyya fi Qanat al-Suwais 1951–1954* (The Secret Resistance in the Suez Canal 1951–1954). Beirut: n.p., 1957.

Tawil, Muhammad al-. *Kaifa Yusna` al-Qarar fi Misr* (How Decisions Are Made in Egypt). Cairo: Star, 1992.

Turabi, Hassan. *Al-Shura wal Dimoqratiyya* (Consultation and Democracy). Khartoum: Dar al-Fikr, n.d.

______. *Al-Haraka al-Islamiyya fil Sudan* (The Islamic Movement in Sudan). Khartoum: n.p., 1990.

Ubaidi, Awni J. al-. *Jama`at al-Ikhwan al-Muslimin Fil Urdun wa Philistine: 1945–1970* (The Muslim Brotherhood Organization in Jordan and Palestine: 1945–1970). Amman: Al-Maktaba al-Wataniyya, 1991.

Yassin, El Sayed, ed. *Al Taqrir al-Istratiji al-`Arabi 1991* (The Arab Strategic Report 1991). Cairo: Markaz al-Dirasat al-Istratijiyya fil Ahram, 1992.

Zaki, Muhammad Shawqi. *Al-Ikhwan al-Muslimun wal Mujtama` al-Masri* (The Muslim Brotherhood and Egyptian Society). Cairo: n.p., 1954.

Personal Interviews

Akailah, Dr. Abdallah al-. Leading Islamist figure. Member of parliament and former Minister of Education. Amman, January 25, 1993.

Akef, Muhammad Faiz. Leading Ikhwan figure and former member of parliament. Cairo, August 13, 1993.

Arabiyat, Dr. Abdullatif. At the time of the interview, Speaker of parliament; current member of the House of Notables. Amman, January 25, 1993.

Farhan, Dr. Ishaq al-. At the time of the interview, member of the House of Notables; current Secretary General of the Islam Action Front. Amman, January 19, 1993.

Hudaibi, Ma'mun al-. Official Ikhwan spokesman and former member of parliament. Cairo, August 11, 1993.
Huwaidi, Fahmi. Independent Islamic writer. Cairo, August 15, 1993.
Khalafat, Fu'ad al-. At the time of the interview, member of parliament. Amman, January 26, 1993.
Qaradawi, Sheikh Yusuf al-. Islamic scholar; leading Islamist figure. Cairo, August 14, 1993.
Qarqar, Dr. Magdi. Assistant Secretary General of the Labor Party. Cairo, August 13, 1993.
Qutb, Muhammad. Islamic scholar; Islamist figure. Makkah, December 13, 1992.
Turabi, Hasan. Islamic scholar; Sudanese Islamist leader. Khartoum, August 8, 1993.

English Newspapers and Periodicals

Civil Society/ Al-Mujtama` al-Madani. Egyptian monthly periodical (English/Arabic).
Keesing's Record of World Events. Monthly periodical, London.
Middle East International. Biweekly periodical, London.
New York Times. US daily newspaper.
Washington Post. US daily newspaper.

Arabic Newspapers and Magazines

Ahali, al-. Egyptian weekly newspaper.
Ahram, al-. Egyptian daily newspaper.
`Amal al-Islami, al-. Islamic Action Front Party newsletter, Jordan.
Da`wa, al-. Egyptian weekly magazine (published temporarily in London).
Dustour, al-. Jordanian daily newspaper.
Gumhurriyya, al-. Egyptian daily newspaper.
Hayat, al-. Arabic daily newspaper (published in London).
Islah. al-. Weekly United Arab Emirates magazine.
Liwa', al-. Jordanian newspaper.
Majalla, al-. Saudi weekly magazine.
Mujtama`, al-. Kuwaiti weekly magazine.
Mujtama` al-Madani, al- /Civil Society. Egyptian monthly periodical (English/Arabic).
Rabat, al-. Jordanian weekly newspaper (discontinued).
Sha`b, al-. Egyptian semi-weekly newspaper.
Sharq al-Awsat, al-. Saudi daily newspaper.
Wafd, al-. Egyptian weekly newspaper.
Wasat, al-. Arabic weekly magazine (published in London).

About the Book and Author

The rise of Islamic movements in the Arab world over the last decade coincided with a move toward democratization throughout the region, yet after hopeful early signs, progress toward democratization has stalled or has even been reversed in all but a few countries. This book explores the linkages between the move to democratize and the Islamist challenge, focusing on the struggle among ruling elites, secularists, and the Islamists to define collective identity—that is, to define what common orientations unite the polity and how disagreements can be addressed, particularly regarding the place of Islam in politics. The author surveys democratization measures since 1980 and analyzes the nature of the Islamist challenge, exploring the factors behind the rise of fundamentalism, the agendas of various Islamic movements, and Islamist concepts of democracy. In a final section the author offers in-depth case studies of Egypt and Jordan.

Najib Ghadbian did his doctoral work at The Graduate School of the City University of New York. He is currently a research analyst for the Emirates Center for Strategic Studies and Research in Abu Dhabi.

Index